The Seven Cs
of Coaching

r

1

7

1

PEARSON
Prentice Hall
BUSINESS

Books that make you better

Books that make you better. That make you *be* better, *do* better, *feel* better. Whether you want to upgrade your personal skills or change your job, whether you want to improve your managerial style, become a more powerful communicator, or be stimulated and inspired as you work.

Prentice Hall Business is leading the field with a new breed of skills, careers and development books. Books that are a cut above the mainstream – in topic, content and delivery – with an edge and verve that will make you better, with less effort.

Books that are as sharp and smart as you are.

Prentice Hall Business.
We work harder – so you don't have to.

For more details on products, and to contact us, visit
www.pearsoned.co.uk

The Seven Cs of Coaching

The definitive guide to collaborative coaching

Mick Cope

PEARSON
Prentice Hall
BUSINESS

Harlow, England • London • New York • Boston • San Francisco • Toronto • Sydney • Tokyo • Singapore
Hong Kong • Seoul • Taipei • New Delhi • Cape Town • Madrid • Mexico City • Amsterdam • Munich • Paris • Milan

PEARSON EDUCATION LIMITED

Edinburgh Gate
Harlow CM20 2JE
Tel: +44 (0)1279 623623
Fax: +44 (0)1279 431059
Website: www.pearsoned.co.uk

First published in Great Britain in 2004
© Mick Cope 2004

ISBN 0 273 68110 9

British Library Cataloguing in Publication Data
A CIP catalogue record for this book can be obtained from the British Library

Library of Congress Cataloging-in-Publication Data
Cope, Mick
   The seven Cs of coaching : the definitive guide to collaborative
coaching / Mick Cope.
      p. cm.
   ISBN 0–273–68110–9 (pbk. : alk. paper)
   1. Executive coaching. I. Title.

HD30.4.C66 2004
658.4'07124--dc22

                                                                2004053533

10 9 8 7 6 5 4 3 2 1
08 07 06 05 04

Designed by Sue Lamble
Typeset in 9pt Stone Serif by 70
Printed and bound in Great Britain by Bell & Bain Ltd, Glasgow

The Publishers' policy is to use paper manufactured from sustainable forests.

For Lin

Go girl go . . .

xxx

Contents

Thanks to . . .

First of all to all the WizOz team for helping to make it happen. In particular Stuart Neath for making the big pitch and getting it off the ground. I can honestly say it might never have happened without you, Stu – cheers mate.

Also Link Motorcycle Training in Chelmsford for a superb experience in being coached – happy to recommend these guys for anyone interested in taking the plunge.

And a big thanks to all the people I have discussed this idea with over recent years and who have knowingly and unknowingly helped in its conception and delivery. A big thanks to Adam Blanch for all his encouragement.

Preface

I've never been a fan of authors who take one formula and milk it dry in book after book. Therefore, after the successful publication of *The Seven Cs of Consulting*, I was slightly concerned about the idea of writing a book that took the principles of 7Cs and applied it to anything else. However, after running numerous courses showing people how to coach more effectively using the 7Cs principles, it became clear that there was added value in taking this route. Let me explain why.

The 7Cs framework was always written on the basis that it offered nothing new in content. What it does offer is a way of packaging and presenting what can be a very complex process in a way that helps people deliver value through sustainable change. The 7Cs framework is nothing more than common sense. But as the adage goes, just because it is common sense it doesn't mean it is common practice. In presenting the model I wanted to codify and simplify a host of very clever and complex models that people learn about but often find difficult to remember.

In addition to the process of codification and simplification I wanted to raise the issue of sustainable value, since research and anecdotal evidence suggested that around 80 per cent of change programmes fail to deliver sustainable change. By including the notion of 'continuance' as a specific step in the life cycle process I hoped to make this more of an addressable topic. I believe this concern is just as pertinent for the issue of coaching as consulting because of the difficulties associated with making personal change stick.

The 7Cs framework is based on a very simple conceptual framework:

1 Understand the person and the problem.

2 Unearth the symptoms and roots of the issue.

3 Generate a solution.

4 Deliver the solution.

5 Make sure it works.

6 Ensure it will be sustainable.

7 Celebrate and say goodbye.

Look to the theories of corporate change – cognitive behavioural therapy, decision theory, total quality, process re-engineering, systems development, etc. – and they all tend to be based around the same generic framework. The benefit of this simple pattern has been further demonstrated by the practical application of the 7Cs in fields as diverse as medical consulting, nursing, corporate security and product pricing teams. The steps in the 7Cs framework are merely based on a set of fundamental truths that form the backbone of any successful client engagement.

However, once *the Seven Cs of Consulting* book had been out for a few years two things surfaced. First, we saw the inexorable rise of coaching as one of the preferred models for personal and corporate change. Second, more and more colleagues were using the 7Cs framework as the basis for their coaching partnerships. However, since the consulting book was biased more towards the corporate market, it made sense to (a) strip out the tools that were less relevant and (b) present a book written specifically for the coach as opposed to the consultant.

My belief is that the 7Cs framework offers a generic set of fundamental principles that will help people to help others help themselves and that these truths are generically applicable to a parent, performance coach or prime minister. If, however, you find that the ideas do not fit, please drop me a line so that we can have a chat and hopefully I can incorporate your suggestions into a future release of the book.

Thanks for taking the time to look at my ideas.

Mick Cope
mick@wizoz.co.uk

1

Introduction: What is coaching?

If you look around at how coaching is currently being described there seems to be a clear polarization into two camps:

1 **Transference:** Those who believe that coaching is a process of transference – whereby one person with prior knowledge or experience can impart this wisdom to others with a goal to optimize performance.

2 **Discovery:** Those who see that the coach's role is to help others release untapped capability – to help the person be who they are and what they want to be. Here the focus is more on releasing potential.

Although people and companies will adopt variations of these forms and use as appropriate, we need to be clear as to the difference between the two camps because of the confusion it can create for the client, coach and corporate leaders. The word coach has become a catchall for a range of roles and positions, some of which might be viewed as more directive in nature while others are more emphatic and supportive in style.

This use of the word 'coach' is common in large companies, for example in call centres where coaching is the term used when a supervisor notices that someone needs to resolve a problem. Other examples might be seen on the Sunday morning football pitch where the coach works with young children to teach them how to take a free kick, or in a fast food restaurant where the supervisor's role is to turn newbies into efficient customer service representatives.

At risk of opening a debate that can never be closed (normally because of semantic interpretation and contextual experiences) I would offer the diagram in Figure 1.1 as a simple representation of the coaching continuum. By no means is this being offered as a definitive model, but it is important that people understand the basis on which the ideas are being presented.

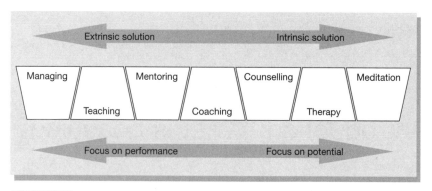

Figure 1.1 Coaching continuum

At the left-hand side we have 'managing' where someone is commanding people to ensure that a specific output is achieved. They will often do this by giving direction and ideas on how the output needs to be delivered. At the other end of the spectrum we have 'meditation' where the idea is to spend time on a contemplative discourse. The person focuses on intrinsic aspects and pays less attention to external forces or solutions. In this sense the value comes from within and is not externally directed or informed.

Please note this is managing – not management. I see managing as a process that people adopt as necessary whereas management might be taken as a role. So the coach might spend most of their time in the central position, but in other cases they might need to move up either end of the spectrum as dictated by the situation. Conversely, a 'manager' might spend the majority of their time in the far left position managing their people, but in some instances may move along the spectrum as dictated by circumstances.

> **I see managing as a process that people adopt as necessary whereas management might be taken as a role.**

The 'managing' end of the spectrum is often more concerned with performance management where the goal is to ensure that the resources or people deliver the expected output. This is akin to buying a car where the top speed is stated as 100mph and ensuring that it can deliver this on demand. In a coaching context this might be the manager who looks after a team of engineers. There is an expected daily rate of jobs that each is targeted to deliver and the manager's role is to ensure that this figure is achieved. Where one of the engineers is below standard the manager might seek to 'coach' them to help bring their output up to scratch.

However, the other end of the spectrum might be more focused on discovering potential. Not just ensuring that the resource will deliver the agreed performance, but rather what this person is capable of – what could it unleash if we were prepared to invest time discovering what latent and tacit talent the person has? – much in the same way that a sports mechanic doesn't seek to get the stated performance from an engine; instead they will invest time, energy and all the talent and years of experience to unearth all the latent power that can be teased from the stock design.

The use of the word coaching in this book is based upon the middle perspective of the coaching continuum. In accepting a coaching engagement the coach will have a material interest in ensuring that the client will deliver the agreed outcome, if not for altruistic reasons, then at least because their personal brand takes a dip every time they coach someone who does not deliver the agreed outcome. At the other end, only the client can deliver change that will add value and be sustainable. Any lasting solution will generally be one that the client discovers, owns and is able to maintain after the coaching engagement has completed.

In bringing these two drivers together, we end up with the following:

- ■ **Coach: '*Help someone*'** – this help might be directive or non-directive based upon the needs of the client, coach and the context where the coaching is taking place.

- ■ **Client: '*to help themselves*'** – this places the ownership squarely on the shoulders of the client and so it is not for the coach to provide or own the solution.

This is why the collaborative nature of the 7Cs framework is so important as it is where these two drivers come together at midpoint on the coaching continuum, as seen in Figure 1.2.

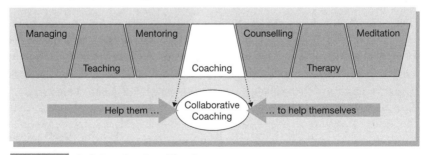

Figure 1.2   Collaborative Coaching fit

The 7Cs framework and associated tools are designed to be used anywhere on this continuum, but the emphasis in the book is related to the coaching point on the continuum where the primary goal is for the coach to help the client to help themselves.

John's journey

In describing the framework, I have also included a running case study of someone who is being coached. The case study draws upon the ideas and models outlined in each chapter and offers an indication of how they might be applied by a coach. My one concern with taking this approach is that it might seem to be offering the 'right' way of using the framework and models. This is certainly not the case. The ideas offered in the book are consciously and deliberately relaxed and adaptable so that people can choose to interpret and deploy them in line with their natural style. Hence, the way that I have described them in the case study will clearly reflect my personal view of the situation and how I might go about it – I am sure that your approach would and should be very different.

The hero of our story is John and he is about to be coached by Julie. The case study picks up from their first meeting and follows them on their journey through to the logical conclusion. It is written to try to highlight both John's and Julie's perspectives and indicate in particular what Julie does to help John and why she makes these particular choices.

Julie is someone who is relatively new to coaching, but she has a real passion for the subject and a real sense of purpose about why it is important for her. She worked for a large company for the early part of her career but then decided to make a life change and travelled round the world for a year to help discover her purpose in life. At the end of this journey she noticed the increasing demand for personal coaching and also recognized the value that such coaching had had for her when thinking about making a life change. So she undertook a study programme, began a coaching practice and now has in the region of ten regular clients.

John is 43, divorced and is a weekend dad with two children. He has worked for the same firm for 19 years but is now faced with the threat of redundancy. He doesn't know for definite, but the rumours are spreading that a downsizing programme will be introduced in the next year. Although he is really scared of leaving, he sees this as the chance to make a break and do some of the things he has been thinking about for the last four years.

At the end of the next chapter we see the point where John meets Julie and they explore the ideas of working together in a coaching partnership.

2

Collaborative Coaching: Introduction

Thus far we have explored the idea that coaching is about 'helping people to help themselves'. This is not a case of the coach 'doing it' to the client. This is a collaborative partnership whereby both players engaged on a shared journey to ensure that the client achieves their perfect picture.

If the coach and client are to collaborate then they need a shared understanding or map of the journey. I am a big fan of maps. Have you ever been the passenger in a car where both you and the driver know where you want to get to but don't have a shared map? They might have a plan of how to get there (or not!) and you probably also have a route you think should be taken. This can (and often does) lead to quite a tense time, with the following emerging:

1 You have to trust they have a route in their head and they're not just guessing.

2 You have to trust that the driver knows the best route (especially if you are heading for a wedding that starts in a few minutes).

3 There can be tension if the driver is less experienced than the passenger.

4 There can be a subtle power battle (note the problem with back seat drivers) as you are putting your life in their hands and just maybe you want to exert some control over the journey.

5 You might believe that the driver is lost, but decide to sit back, arrive at the wedding late and then wallow in the pleasure of blaming the failure on them.

6 There can be different interpretations in the directions – does turn left at the roundabout mean first exit, left as the crow flies or left off the slip road as you leave the roundabout?

Since driver and passenger don't have a common platform by which to have a conversation, the relationship can be fraught with problems. Imagine how much simpler it can be when both have a simple map in front of them – a chart that indicates where they are, where they are going and the route they will follow to get there.

I would suggest that when the coach and client don't have a shared framework the same issues would arise and in many cases lead to abandoned outcomes that leave both players worse for wear. For example, imagine the coach and client who are working together without any common map or language:

1 The client has to trust the coach and hope they are not bluffing.

2 The client has to trust that the coach knows the best approach to help resolve their concern (especially if being interviewed for promotion in a few weeks).

3 There can be tension if the coach is less experienced than the client.

4 There can be a subtle power battle as the client might be putting their career or personal life in the hands of the coach and just maybe the client wants to exert some control over the journey.

5 The client might believe that the coach is wrong, but decides to sit back, fail their interview and then wallow in the pleasure of blaming the failure on them.

6 There can be different interpretations in the directions being offered – does 'take a risk in your life' mean smile at a stranger, swim a wild river or resign from your current job?

The Collaborative Coaching framework aims to help address many of the issues raised – not by giving a solution but by giving both client and coach the shared language by which they can agree the journey to be taken, allowing sensible conversations to occur through a shared language and offering the client a greater say in the way their coaching engagement is managed.

❝ There can be tension if the coach is less experienced than the client. ❞

Choosing the choice

Once the idea of coaching as a managed process of helping is clear, we can start to understand how this help is offered. Clearly coaching is being used in a multiplicity of places and many of the broad coaching themes can be seen below:

- Spend less
- Earn more
- Save more
- Become financially secure
- Change careers
- Get promoted
- Reduce work hours
- Reduce travel time
- Improve specific skills
- Create work schedule
- Do work that is authentic
- Reduce stress
- Improve health

- Improve a relationship
- Find a new relationship
- Close a relationship
- Become more assertive
- Generate revenue
- Manage conflict
- Grow self-esteem
- Make better life choices
- Make a big life change
- Reduce addictive tendency
- Manage self-motivation
- Define new strategies
- Boost personal productivity

One common theme sits under all of these coaching topics – someone acts in a certain way and they want to feel, think or behave differently. Having recognized that their current journey does not get them where they want to be, they need to alter the journey – and the coach is there as a partner to help them deliver a change that will stick.

We may liken this to Figure 2.1, where the person is following a direction but then reaches a choice point where they decide to alter the route and do something different. So the smoker chooses to give up smoking; the team member decides to get promoted; or the person with low self-esteem decides to make a change in how they view themselves. All of these examples indicate someone who wants to change their journey and hence the end destination. However, the moment this change in direction takes place, a rubber band will kick in to try to pull the client back to the original trajectory. The new team leader yearns to give up all their new responsibilities and be one of the team again, the born-again runner wants to stay in bed, and the newly assertive manager tries to avoid confrontation and go back to being nice to people.

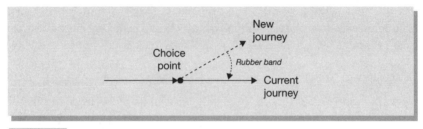

Figure 2.1   Choice point

The coach's role is to help them (a) make the change in their journey and (b) stick with the new direction – even when times get tough and they yearn for the comfort of the old way they knew and understood. It is important for both coach and client to understand that there will be forces that strive to pull the client back into the comfort zone. Like a huge rubber band that tugs incessantly, the tension between sticking with the new and reverting to the old is always there.

❝ The tension between sticking with the new and reverting to the old is always there. ❞

The coach and client need to consider the nature of the tension and how it may impact the sustainability of the planned change. One way to do this is to look at the change and the angle of deviation from their normal path. Is the client after help with a relatively small deviation from the norm, such as correcting a faulty golf swing or helping to fine-tune their presentation skills? Or is the deviation more of a major diversion, where the client wants to completely change how they operate, to the point that it might be viewed as a complete reversal in direction? This might be the smoker who wants to quit, the senior executive who plans to give it all up and open an almond farm in Spain, or the committed atheist who wants to seek a faith. All these are significant redirections that require pretty serious support and understanding from the coach.

As we think about this idea of redirection and the level of deviation from the established patterns, it can help to map the angle of change using the following examples:

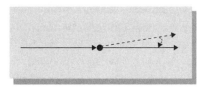

Divert

In this case the angle of deviation is marginal and will have a relatively small level of impact on the person and their life. This might be akin to someone who wants to improve their time management skills. Because the energy is still broadly in the same direction with just a slight deviation, there will be a relatively low amount of energy in the rubber band as it tries to pull the client back to the old habits. However, because the gap is so narrow, drift can occur as people slip into old behaviours without realizing it. When the manager misses one goal-setting session it is not noticed, but they then miss it for a week and then a month, until eventually the behaviour has reverted to the original direction.

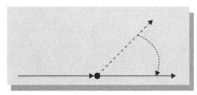

Corner

This is where someone makes a significant change and turns a corner in how they want to behave. In this case, the change has a larger deviation than a simple diversion from the normal behaviour. This might be the debt-ridden compulsive spender who decides they want to buy clothes only once a month and from a budget store. The shift from the norm (for the habitual fashion shopper) is quite large. The rubber band will kick in a lot more heavily (especially as they walk past their favourite high street store).

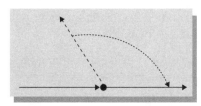

Break

In this case the change is a significant variation from the normal direction. This might be likened to the person who plans to get fit by spending time at the gym. Hence time normally spent watching TV now has to be given over to exercising. The rubber band is really kicking in now, as every time they have to go to the gym each step is full of pain as the TV screams at them to stay at home and relax. In this case drift will be quite obvious because the new action is directionally different from the established behaviours.

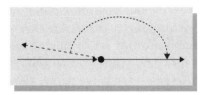

About turn

This is a major change in direction, where the new action is the complete opposite to the old behaviours. This is what happened when I decided to give up drink. This was a complete reversal away from my established comfort zone. At first the emotional, mental and physical energy required to counter the pull of the rubber was quite draining. But over time the band lost its energy and I was able to maintain the velocity and momentum of the new direction with some ease.

By working together on these issues the coach can agree with the client what action they will take to help ensure that the rubber band does not snap into place and cause reversion to the comfort zone.

Hence when first working with a new client it is pertinent and important to consider:

1   What is their current direction?

2   What is the new direction they wish to take?

3   How different is the new from the current (degree of variation)?

4   How strong will the reversion rubber band be?

5   How strong are the forces pulling someone in the new direction?

In many ways the role of the coach here is twofold: first to help cut the old rubber band and second to anchor a new one that pulls the person in the desired direction, as seen in Figure 2.2. Once they are confident that the old band has been eliminated and that the new one is exercising sufficient pull in the new direction, in many ways the coach's job is done.

The 7Cs framework is carefully designed to offer a collaborative framework that will help deliver these two processes. Through building trust, giving feedback, challenging perceptions, highlighting limiting beliefs and

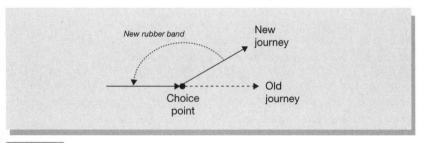

Figure 2.2   New rubber band

surfacing shadows the coach is able to cut the rubber band that pulls the client in the unwanted direction. Then, using techniques such as directional setting, creativity tools, rich measures, choice management and planned withdrawal processes, the coach can help the client lock in the new rubber band and so eliminate the risk of reversion.

John's journey

After the introductions and questions, Julie asks John to explain about himself and to give an introduction to the thing he would like coaching on. At this point Julie is not looking for detail, depth or a decision on whether to take John on as a client. She just wants to understand the nature of the issue that he requires help on and in particular the degree of change that he will need to make and sustain.

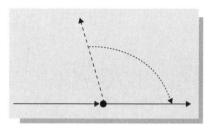

Choice angle

John briefly describes his background and the fact that he has worked for 19 years for a large petroleum company, for the last ten as a manager. He describes how redundancy may be looming and how this will give him a chance to make a change that he has often thought about. Julie talks briefly about the issues of redundancy, but then moves to ask John about the goal of what he would like to achieve. He describes how for many years he has been dabbling with the idea of becoming a personal fitness trainer. He has always been interested in sports and has kept himself fit. He has been doing some background studying around the technical areas of health and fitness and would be keen to gain a qualification in this area.

At this point Julie is interested in working with John, but she first needs to understand the nature of the choice that John wants help with and in particular the strength of the two rubber bands. She needs to understand what forces will be acting on him as he attempts to make such a change.

After a ten-minute conversation Julie begins to see that the forces pulling John to this new way of life are a desire for freedom, a wish to turn a hobby into a living and the idea that he would be able to spend more time with his children. Conversely, the forces that would pull him back into staying with the current firm are the need for security to pay the mortgage, the kids' schooling and university fees, and the strong company pension plan.

Julie spends some time talking with John about these two opposing forces and in particular how the shape of his choice angle (about-turn) means that he would face considerable pressure to either remain in his current job or give up the dream and get another job as a mechanic somewhere else.

She feels that John is serious about the desire to change, but before agreeing to a coaching contract wants to understand further both what he wants to achieve at the end of the change and why he has come to her for help.

3

Coaching foundations

Before we consider the seven stages in the Collaborative Coaching framework, it is important to provide some underpinning to the model. These core factors are the basic precepts that both drive the coaching model and ensure that it does not fall into the trap of being this year's fad (as this is a real risk). Two issues need to be understood:

- The purpose of coaching – why we do it and what we seek to achieve.
- The pillars of coaching – what the coach looks for in the client.

These two areas are easily skipped over in the rush to 'fix the problem', but experience has shown that successful and sustainable coaching is driven by a willingness to embrace and understand these factors.

The purpose and pillars are key because they drive the questions that you might ask the client prior to committing to a relationship with them.

Collaborative Coaching purpose

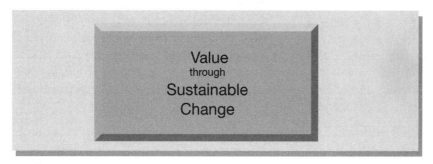

Figure 3.1 The delivery of value

It really is quite simple – coaching is about the delivery of value through sustainable change (Figure 3.1):

- Change – something must be different at the end of the coaching process. The coach and client must always define and agree what that something will be. If the client doesn't think, feel or behave any differently at the end of the coaching process then what is the point of the investment in time and energy? It is the need to specify the exact change that is desired which underpins the whole coaching engagement.

- Value – people hold the gain when they focus on the value derived from the change rather than the change itself. The client must focus less on the change and place more emphasis on the value derived from the change and its potential for sustainability. For someone being coached to deal with their low self-esteem, the emphasis initially needs to be on the change, i.e. reducing the low self-esteem, but potentially more important is the value they will derive from the change, i.e. the chance to gain promotion.

- Sustainability – coaching that doesn't last isn't coaching. The best (and ethical) coach is the one who enables the client to fly solo and not be dependent on them at the end of the engagement. This is the root problem with so many coaching engagements. The coach and client have a great time, make amazing strides in performance, celebrate their success and then move on, only to find that any value added is eroded 3–6 months later. Consider changes where people try to lose weight, give up smoking, and get fit: they all start with great intentions but so often fail to deliver sustainable change.

However, of the three factors, too much emphasis is often placed on the change area and not enough on the other two. At the end of the day change is relatively easy. The smoker can stop smoking for a week, managers can reduce work hours for a month, or people can boost their self-esteem for a few weeks. But once this short and seductive period of exhilaration is over, the daily grind sets back in and the smoker reaches for a cigarette at the next point of stress, the manager finds a reason to stay late at work, and the low self-esteem surfaces when someone points out that your tie looks stupid with the suit you are wearing.

❝ At the end of the day change is relatively easy. ❞

Only where the change, value and sustainability have been fully addressed can the coach walk away with some satisfaction at having delivered an ethical and responsible service.

Coaching pillars

Two of the questions that the coach must always ask is 'why me?' and 'why now?'. Why has this person come to me for coaching and what sits behind their intention for change? The three pillars that the coach must always seek to test are the client's level of invitation, intent and independence (Figure 3.2):

■ **Invitation:** The coach must be invited to help the client and cannot simply launch themselves on to someone uninvited like some crusading knight intent on making life better for the other person. As the adage goes you can lead a horse to water but you can't make it drink. I can 'coach' someone until I am blue in the face, but unless they want to be coached all I am doing is probably wasting my time and theirs. A situation where the coach chooses to 'coach' someone because 'they obviously need it' is not Collaborative Coaching. Hence it is not practical for someone's line manager to assume that they can coach a team member. Where this does happen, in most cases the team member will simply play along with the manager's help, but will still end up sticking to their original thoughts, feelings and behaviours. The coach must ensure that the client is there of their free will and is not coming along just to satisfy others' needs or to play a 'look good' faking game.

■ **Intent:** Serious is as serious does – coaching is about doing, not just talking about doing. The coach must be confident that the client wants to change, wants to realize a benefit from the change, and importantly really wants the change to last, even when there is no one around to offer a crutch. A key part of this intent is to test whether they are serious about dealing with issues that have caused the problem in the first place. The smoker might be smoking for a reason that has little to do with the addiction to nicotine; the bullying manager might behave in this way for reasons that they are scared of surfacing. The coach must determine whether the client is willing to delve into the areas that might be at the root of any issues. The final test of seriousness is to be sure that they are prepared to stick to the change without any ongoing support from the coach. The coach's goal is to test and ensure that the client has fully committed to the change before closing the engagement. If the engagement commences without the intent being stated and tested, the partnership is potentially doomed to failure at some point down the road.

■ **Independence:** The role of the coach is to help the client help themselves – not to do it for them. However, anyone who has tried to help someone else will understand the deep temptation to just do it for them. When the other person struggles to understand something, can't find the time, finds it difficult or is close to tears with frustration, it can seem the right thing to put out a hand and ease their pain by doing it for them. But most coaching interventions are dealing with some type of addictive behaviour. This might be a narcotic or nicotine addition, or a warm bed on a Sunday morning. At some point the addict has to learn to go it alone and fight their own battle. If the coach is always there to fight the battle for them, the client never gets a chance to play the game and find out whether they will be able to fly solo once the coach disappears.

The coach must aspire to keep their hands off and let the client be hands on, even when the temptation to fix it for them is so strong that it seems unbearable. A change of any kind is more likely to be sustainable if the person affected by the change has taken ownership and responsibility for it. In a coaching scenario our aim is to avoid the client saying things like: 'I only went along with that because you suggested it' or 'Well, I was not really convinced that it would work anyway.' Both the coach and client need to be aware that there will come a point when the dependency will be cut and the client must be confident of standing on their own. If they still need the coach after the process is over, that is not coaching – it is managing. The coach must therefore test this conditional factor from the outset. Is the client looking for a short-term comfort blanket or are they really prepared to fly the nest without the coach and achieve self-maintained improvement?

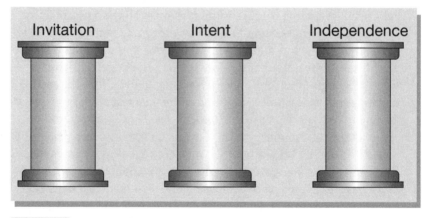

Figure 3.2   Coaching pillars

It might not always be possible to get confirmation that each of the three pillars is in place, but a failure to even check and consider them means that a short-term and possibly less than ethical approach is being taken to the engagement. The pillars are like gates that the client needs to get through before the coach should really consider taking them on as a client. They might not pass all three tests with a distinction, but there should really be evidence of some desire to give the relationship a fighting chance of delivering sustainable value.

Once the coach has a degree of confidence in the client and their desire to achieve a sustainable outcome, the next stage is how to develop a robust coaching relationship. Although there are many factors to consider at this point, one of the foundation stones will be the coach's ability to develop a high level of trust with the client. This is the oil that lubricates the relationship and can make the difference between one that fails to deliver sustainable value and one that slips effortlessly through the various stages of the 7Cs framework.

> **“ One of the foundation stones will be the coach's ability to develop a high level of trust with the client. ”**

Coaching questions

Some of the questions that the coach might ask before and during the coaching process in relationship to the foundations are:

- What is the change you wish to make?
- What triggered the desire to take action?
- Why is this important to you?
- How will things be different once we have completed the engagement?
- What will be the benefit for you in making the change?
- What will be the benefit for others?
- How long do you want the change to last for?
- Have you tried this type of thing before?
- Why do you want to make this change?
- What value do you believe I can add?
- Have you spoken with other coaches to see how they might offer help?
- How would you define coaching?
- What would be your reaction if I said I didn't believe I could help you?

- Why is this important to you?
- When the coaching engagement is over, do you foresee any problems in maintaining the change?
- What do you think my role is in helping you with the change?
- How many hours a week are you prepared to put into this (outside of our meetings)?

John's journey

Before agreeing to the contract Julie wanted to understand a number of things about John and the help he expected from her.

The first questions she raised were designed to understand more about the change he wanted to make. She challenged him to define the specific change, how he would be different as a

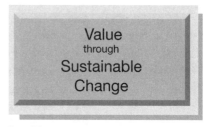

Coaching purpose

result of the coaching, and what help she could offer. Although John's view was slightly muddy, after some discussion he was able to explain that the key change would be in his ability to operate as a free agent and not be reliant on a parent organization to look after him. So the change would be about self-sufficiency in a free market.

Once this was clear and Julie felt comfortable that she could in fact help John to achieve this, the next conversation revolved around the value that this would bring to his life. Her key question was, 'What benefit will achieving this give you?' John's view was that the value for him would be in the ability to look after his family without having to worry about a boss threatening redundancy in future years.

The final challenge, and one that Julie found that potential clients often struggle with, was around the notion of sustainability. She pressed John to convince her that he would stick through the difficult times and not give in at the first pain of change. In particular she was looking for evidence of previous examples where he had maintained a chosen course in difficult times. She was pleased that he was able to talk about recent studies he had undertaken at night school. They had been difficult because of work and family commitments, but because they were important he persisted and achieved a commendable result.

The final three areas she wanted to understand were based around the three pillars of intervention, intent and independence. John was able to help her with this as he explained that no one had pushed him to seek help from a coach. He chose it partly from reading case studies where it had worked in the

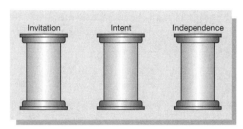

Coaching pillars

sports field but also because he used the idea of coaching with apprentices at work and found that it made a difference to the way they developed. Satisfied that the invitation and intent were clear, John then helped her with the final pillar by explaining that he had mapped a clear outline of how long the programme would last and what his next development steps would be.

At this point Julie was satisfied that John was a client in whom she would be proud to invest her time, energy and brand and so an initial coaching contract was agreed.

4

Up close and personal – grow the trust fund

The problem with trust is that it's like a good partnership – you know it when you see it, but it's hard to define the specific factors. As an example, think about someone you know well and trust implicitly. What is it that makes you think of that person? What do they and you do to maintain the relationship? Now think of another person you know just as well but don't trust. Consider what it is that each of you does to create a relationship lacking in substance and value. What's the impact of such a relationship and what overheads or implicit costs does it impose? If you ask them to do a job or help you out, to what extent do you have to give up valuable personal time to check and oversee the work? Do you lose sleep because there is a fear in the back of your mind that they might not deliver on time?

The time that the client and coach spend with each other is an investment process, where each chooses to offer and donate their personal resources and capital to create social capital. Coaching partnerships are like savings accounts – we put time and energy into them in the hope that a return on investment will occur.

Managing your investment

There is a simple model of trust that can be used to measure and manage the nature of a relationship:

1 **T**ruthful – the extent to which integrity, honesty and truthfulness are developed and maintained.

2 **R**esponsive – the openness, mental accessibility or willingness to share ideas and information freely.

3 **U**niform – the degree of consistency, reliability and predictability contained within the relationship.

4 **S**afe – the loyalty, benevolence or willingness to protect, support and encourage each other.

5 **T**rained – the competence, technical knowledge and capabilities of both parties.

Where these five attributes are soundly in place, the coaching relationship might be deemed to be in credit. Where one or more of the factors is diminished or missing, it's possible the relationship is moving into a debit state.

It can be very easy to move the account sliders on the account into credit or debit, as seen in Figure 4.1. When working with a client you only have to give a false reason for being late one day to weaken the 'Truthful' slider; ignore some of their requests for help for them to feel that you're not being 'Responsive'; tell them different things at different times to upset the 'Uniform' balance; be indiscreet about someone else to raise concerns about how safe they feel sharing personal issues; or appear not to be competent in the questioning process to reduce the value in the 'Trained' sub-account. Slippage in any one area of the trust fund erodes the value of the total trust fund and even worse reduces the opportunity to help deliver sustainable value.

> **❝ Slippage in any one area of the trust fund erodes the value of the total trust fund. ❞**

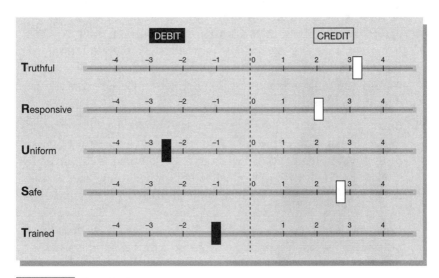

Figure 4.1 Trust fund

When considered in a coaching context, the trust factors might be described as follows:

- **Truthful:** Both the coach and the client have a responsibility to be honest with each other. When entering into a collaborative coaching partnership it is very easy to tell the other person what they want to hear. However, in most cases the truth will out. Once either party realizes that the other has been less than truthful all the good work will come undone.

- **Responsive:** This refers to the coach's desire to focus on the client's world and suspend their own needs. By understanding the client's world they can be 'with' them as a whole person and not just pick up on partial signals offered during the coaching session. In practice, demonstration of responsiveness can be verbal restatements of the client's emotions: facial expression of acceptance, such as smiling; body posture that shows interest in the client's world, such as leaning forward; the use of eye contact; not taking direct notes when they are talking; nodding or a soft tone of voice that does not seek to subdue or outdo the client's tonal volume or quality.

- **Uniform:** Much of the implicit value from the coach/client relationship comes from repetition. Because the coach and client meet on a regular basis they are able to build on previous trust deposits and so develop a stronger compound relationship. However, the moment that the coach is not consistent in their language and behaviour then doubt will be triggered. Nowhere is this more evident than in the parent/child relationship. When parents are consistent in their behaviour children learn to count on that parent and will feel more secure in their relationship. Once the parent starts to become inconsistent in how they treat the child then this creates confusion, dissent and distrust.

- **Safe:** Establishment of a safe environment for the client is paramount in the development of the other four trust levers. Unless the client really believes that the coach will not harm them physically, mentally or emotionally, any interaction will be constrained and cloaked in a protective veil. However, it can be difficult to explicitly determine what factors will make the client feel 'safe'. For some, safety might come from working with a coach who has shared similar experiences; for others it can be a formal contract of non-disclosure; in other cases it might be the use of a coach who has no contact with the people in the client's current work area. Often the simplest way is to ask the client what would help them feel safe in the relationship and then check this out on a regular basis to confirm that the client feels secure.

▦ **Trained:** Think about any life situation where you seek help or development from another person. One of the key prerequisites might be clear demonstration of the person's knowledge and competence. This might be in the content area, i.e. do they have sufficient knowledge of the area to have a sensible conversation about the topic being addressed? Or it might be process competence, i.e. do they know how to coach? The important thing is for the coach to understand what the client needs to trust them and then to offer the necessary evidence in the early stage of the coaching relationship.

Consider the various factors that can deliver credits and debits:

	Debit	*Credit*
Table 4.1 **Credits and debits**		
Truthful	▦ Lie about the reason for being late to a meeting. ▦ Give positive feedback to the client when they clearly know that it isn't warranted.	▦ Share thoughts on last session including what went well and what didn't seem to be so effective. ▦ Accept when a mistake is made and be open about it.
Responsive	▦ Take a phone call part way through the coaching session. ▦ Keep looking at the clock to see how long is left in the session.	▦ Take time to prepare before meeting the client by reading previous session notes. ▦ Accept that the client can have operational priorities that take precedence over the coaching session.
Uniform	▦ Let personal moods drive behaviour – so one meeting is upbeat and the next downbeat. ▦ Show incongruence by smiling with the mouth and not the voice.	▦ Keep clear and consistent notes that don't vary across the session. ▦ Use consistent language throughout the session.
Safe	▦ Bad-mouth other clients. ▦ Leave notes of the session on a desk in an open room.	▦ Refuse to talk about what happens in other clients' sessions and keep all paperwork locked away. ▦ Don't vary from the contracted process without agreeing with the client.

Table 4.1	Continued	
	Debit	*Credit*
Trained	■ Don't have a professional manner and process. ■ Don't listen properly.	■ Offer demonstrable evidence of previous coaching experience and successes. ■ Ask the appropriate questions without mind-reading the client's views.

When the coach enters into a coaching partnership the client is entrusting their whole being to them. The client is saying, 'here I am offering this gift of "me", please look after it in all your dealings'. When acting as a coach you must be acutely conscious of the extent to which you are dealing with a gift that you have been entrusted with and all the explicit and implicit responsibilities that go with this role.

Coaching questions

Truthful
■ How do you feel the last session went?
■ Is there anything I have been doing that might cause offence or worry you?

Responsive
■ What would you like to cover at the meeting?
■ What is important for you when we meet?

Uniform
■ Is there anything that I do differently when we meet that might cause confusion?
■ Is there any language I use that confuses you?

Safe
■ Is there anything I can do to make you feel more comfortable when we meet?
■ How do you want to deal with information that might be super-sensitive?
■ What would you like to include in the coaching contract?

Trained
■ Would you like me to outline my experience in this field?

John's journey

Julie was pleased that the contract with John had been established. She was then keen to develop a high-trust working relationship as quickly as possible so that she could commence the diagnostic process.

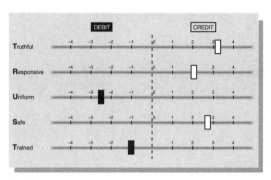

Trust fund

To aid this Julie suggested that she meet with John – just for a coffee and general chat to get to know each other. Julie had two goals with this session. First, to get closer to John and begin to build a level of rapport. Second, to explicitly talk to John about the need for trust in their relationship and agree how they could work to grow the level of the trust fund they shared.

Julie spent some time sharing the trust fund framework with John. This offered three important benefits. First, it gave them a shared language to talk about trust as an explicit topic and moved it into an arena where it could be talked about in the open. Second, it demonstrated that Julie was not afraid of climbing inside the deeper issues that are needed to help sustain a successful coaching partnership. Finally, it modelled the style and approach that Julie would be using under the Collaborative Coaching banner – namely 'teaching the coaching process precedes applying the coaching process'.

5

Collaborative Coaching process

It is important to stress from the outset that this is a framework, not a methodology. It is not designed to be a regimented process that needs to be followed religiously. The idea is to offer a pattern that people can follow as and when appropriate. So the coach and client make the choices of where to go on the journey and what tools to use rather than some detached author sitting miles and miles away (hopefully in the sun).

The idea behind the coaching framework is to help ensure that the client is involved in the choice process. For example, one of my big frustrations in life is working with 'professionals' (doctors, accountants, solicitors, plumbers, etc.). I am always sure that they know what they are doing, but rarely do they share how they are going to do it. As professionals they have a client management process (implicit or explicit) and in their head they are being effective by following an expert and ethical process. The trouble is that I don't know what that process is! If I don't understand it, how can I know whether it is being followed, how can I make choices about its validity for my content and context, and how can I voice an opinion if I want to do something different?

By the very fact that the client process is not shared, I am automatically placed into a position of subordination and dependency. Think how you feel when you see the plumber or doctor and they give the sharp intake of breath. You know there is a problem but have no idea how they arrived at the decision and whether the analysis is valid. As such you are placed in the role of sacrificial lamb laid out for the slaughter. The dependency starts the moment you meet them, and even when they have left you are still dependent and emotionally or commercially hooked for the next time you need help.

The Collaborative Coaching model is built on the premise that the coach will always teach the framework before they seek to coach with it. This focus on the role of teacher helps in a number of ways. First, it ensures that both coach and client will have a shared understanding of the process to be followed. Second, it helps to transfer responsibility for managing the coaching process and associated outcome to the client. Finally, it should ensure that the client is able to self-coach and hence is not reliant on the coach to ensure that the change is sustainable.

The framework in summary

The framework is a seven-stage pattern that follows the themes shown in Figure 5.1. Within each of the seven stages in the wheel is a range of tools and techniques that help expand the diagnostic process. Again, the idea behind the tools is not that they are definitive solutions or that they should be followed religiously. The seven stages can be described as follows:

❝ The idea behind the tools is not that they are definitive solutions. ❞

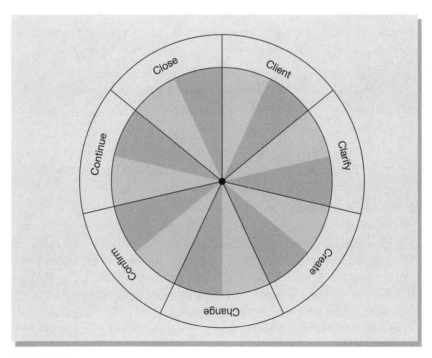

Figure 5.1 Collaborative Coaching wheel

1 **Client:** From the outset the coach will seek to ensure that the whole person is explored by understanding the client's emotional, logical and behavioural drivers. Once the person is clearly understood, the coach will seek to understand the topic that the client wishes to address. They will consider what has happened, what is happening and what the client wants to happen. They will want to understand the broad issues, the pragmatic factors and the microelements that need to be taken into account to ensure success. The framework uses two models at this stage:

- The '3D ME' humanistic model that underpins how we all feel, think and behave.

- The 'MPH' mapping tool that helps to extract the whole story from the client and not just those aspects they prefer to offer.

2 **Clarify:** The coach must be able to get beneath the client's skin to really understand what is going on. This framework seeks to deal with this by addressing two factors: what are the blocks and barriers that the client has created in the form of limiting beliefs? Second, what are the undiscussable issues that exist between the coach and the client? What is it that the client is not telling the coach and how might these shadow issues impact the outcome of the engagement? The coach must always seek to climb inside the client's world and not be prepared to be shrugged off when they feel that the questioning is getting difficult.

The two primary tools used in this stage are:

- The 'Fantasy Ladder', which helps to map and manage any limiting beliefs that the client might have about themselves.

- The 'Shadow Map', which helps the client to explore what undiscussable issues might exist in the relationship and how these might be surfaced without too much pain.

3 **Create:** There will always be time pressure in any coaching relationship. Both coach and client are busy people and the partnership is only a small element in a very busy life. It is this pressure to fix that can cause the client to seek out instant answers, and deliver quick solutions that can get the problem sorted so that they can get on with things. The coach has a strong role here to help the client consider new ways to solve old problems and, once the solution is identified, to then test and ensure that the choice is an optimum one and not a rushed or less-than-optimum solution.

The two aspects considered at this stage are:

■ The CREATE framework, which is a simple but robust tool that helps the client look for diverse options and then helps manage the solution selection process.

■ The CHOICE model, which offers a powerful framework that will help the client consider the cost and consequences of the proposed solution and ensure that they are using the optimum solution and one that will deliver sustainable value.

4   **Change:** Once the diagnosis is complete and the solution is established, the client will be put under real pressure. Until this point everything is conceptual and the client can talk about what they are 'going' to do. At some stage they will have to 'do'. It is at this point they have to move out of the comfort zone of planning and really start to address what change they will need to make to achieve the desired outcome. The driving force at this stage may well have to come from the coach. This might be empathic or soft support to help encourage the client through the change or at the other end of the spectrum having to take a more commanding presence to drive the change.

   Two core models are considered here:

■ The Y-Curve considers how people go through change and how even the smallest of changes (even self-imposed) can result in either dissent or loss of motivation which in turn can trigger resistance.

■ The CHANGE framework addresses the issue around mobilization in the coaching partnership and explores the level of force or control that the coach might agree to apply.

5   **Confirm:** There is a natural human tension that means we are often scared to stand on the scales at the end of a week's dieting. Who really wants to face that pain of finally realizing that things haven't gone so well this week? As humans we almost instinctively seem to find ways to avoid the measurement process. However, measurement is a powerful process when used in a positive way. Sometimes you have to be brave and look under the bed in order to find out that there are no monsters lying in wait. The two models considered in this stage are:

■ The idea of 'Cockpit confirmation' – or developing the client's capability to self-monitor and measure their level of achievement.

■ The 'F-Games' model, which considers the games that people play when faced with the need to look in the mirror and honestly measure themselves.

6 **Continue:** There is no feeling like putting on that comfortable pair of old shoes. You have worn them for years and they have always served well. One day you decide to change and invest in a new pair. After a day or two your feet ache as the new leather fails to bend to the way you walk and you decide to go back to the old shoes just to save your aching feet. It is this natural resistance to new ways of thinking, feeling and behaving that often kills the engagement. The coach and client must counteract this repressive force with a positive one. The two themes are:

■ The notion of 'Buckets and Balloons' and how to identify those things that will cause decay in the change and those things that will help it to last.

■ The metaphor of 'Miracle Mountain' and the fact that people often look for miracle solutions and are not prepared to make the necessary investment to deliver sustainable change.

7 **Close:** Finally, you have just spent the last six months running a gruelling project at work that has really taken its toll on your work and home life. You are sure that everything is wrapped up and complete. You are so confident that when one of the team suggests that you run a closure workshop to dot the Is and cross the Ts you politely tell them to take a hike. The job is done so now everyone can go on holiday. This is a natural process of coming down from a big high. The trouble is that you have to resist this pressure to ignore the last element because that is where the learning takes place, the value is realized and any hidden problems are identified. The positive force required at this stage is one of perseverance, just to hold on to the end and celebrate the success of the change. Two key themes are considered here:

> **❝ This is a natural process of coming down from a big high. ❞**

■ The need to help the client 'Look Back and Learn' – so as to ensure that the outcome has been delivered and that learning has been gleaned along the way, both of which will have a profound impact on the sustainability of the change.

■ Collaborative Coaching is founded on the principle of sustainable change not short-lived satisfaction. As such the coach must test to ensure that the client is able to 'Fly Solo' before disengaging and moving on.

These seven stages and 14 tools form the Collaborative Coaching model seen in Figure 5.2.

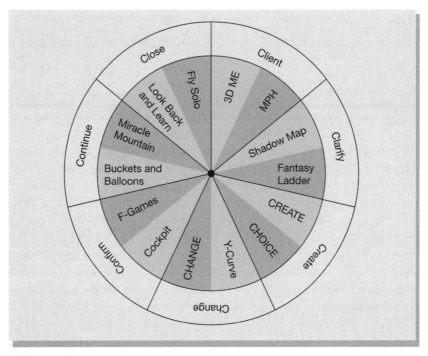

Figure 5.2 Full Collaborative Coaching framework

In the rest of the book we will go through each of the stages and tools on a step-by-step basis. A key part of each stage will be the questions presented at the end. Again, the questions should not be seen as the 'right' way of doing it, they are just questions you might use. Successful coaching will be based on your ability to internalize the tools and frame questions that work for you and help the client – not simply use the stock or standard questions that are included in the book.

Following the framework

In essence the Collaborative Coaching idea uses a seven-stage model where each stage consist of two core tools. This gives us the following tools to use when working with a client:

Client	Clarify	Create	Change	Confirm	Continue	Close
▥ 3D ME	▥ Fantasy ladder	▥ CREATE	▥ Y-Curve	▥ Cockpit	▥ Buckets and Balloons	▥ Look Back and Learn
▥ MPH	▥ Shadow Map	▥ CHOICE	▥ CHANGE	▥ F-Games	▥ Miracle Mountain	▥ Fly Solo

In considering these various stages and models it is important to reinforce that the Collaborative Coaching pattern is not a mechanistic, linear, sequential pattern. It is not a case that you start at stage 1 with tool one and work your way religiously around the framework. The model is and never ever should be a rigid methodology that has to be followed. It is there as a framework that should aid the process rather than drive it. Because of this there is no right start point (you could start the coaching journey at any stage), there is no right tool (use any tool in any stage and if the tool doesn't work then throw it away and use one that does), and the framework is not bounded (these are just 'some' tools, not 'the' tools).

Be prepared to experiment and play with the stages, the tools and the order in which they are applied. The whole point of having a shared framework is to aid the collaborative process, so that either client or coach can suggest a diversion and if the diversion proves fruitless, it is easy to return to the original start point. If the client starts off by saying, 'I have a big problem', ask them, 'How do you know?' In this way you are making a choice to start at the Confirm stage – because that seems to be where the client is starting. If, however, they start by saying, 'I can never get this thing to work', the suggestion is that they have naturally moved to the Continue stage – so stick with them. Ask them about the times when it hasn't worked, why it hasn't worked and what the real issue might be. Doing this allows you to naturally move into the Client stage and so begin a deeper diagnostic process.

> **❝ Be prepared to experiment and play with the stages. ❞**

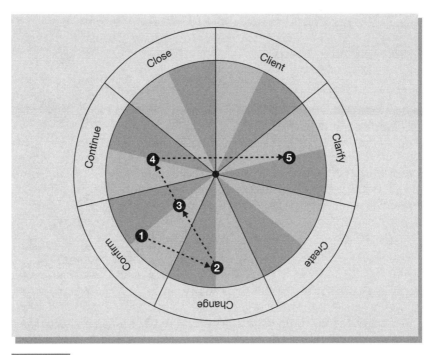

Figure 5.3   Flexible flow

For example, in Figure 5.3 the coach and client have spent the first part of the engagement focusing on a range of tools from the backend of the wheel. The flow went something like: (1) What makes you think you have a problem? (2) What is the change you tried to make? (3) How do you know it didn't work? (4) How long did it last for? (5)Why do you think it didn't work?

John's journey

Taking the principle indicated in the previous section that education precedes action – Julie now sought to help John understand the journey they would be embarking on.

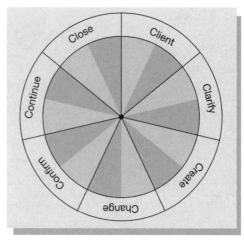

7Cs wheel

Julie built this around a three-stage approach. The first stage was to give John a series of questions to think about prior to a meeting. These questions are designed to put the onus on the client to think through and prepare thoroughly for the first coaching session. (NB: this set of questions can be found in the Client Pre-work section later in the book.) John found the questions really challenging and felt that he could answer properly only 75 per cent of them. For Julie this was fine because John spent time thinking about the issues and uncovering the questions he couldn't answer, thus helping her to understand areas where exploratory time should be allocated.

The second stage was to take John through an overview of the 7Cs model. At this stage all Julie focused on was the outline model; she did not get into the specific tools that might be applied in each of the stages. John felt that this description really helped him to understand what he would be doing within the coaching engagement. What encouraged Julie was the fact that John was a willing and able student, but also he challenged the model and questioned why certain topics were being covered and why others were not included.

The final stage was to build an engagement plan using the 7Cs framework. The idea was to establish an outline structure of what stages would be covered and when. By doing this they were able to anticipate the likely meeting dates and duration. On a practical level this allowed John to match any key points in the process with his personal diary so as to ensure that he would not be in a position where he would need to cancel a meeting because of work commitments.

6

Client – understand the person and the picture

The story so far

At this stage of the coaching partnership two key things have been established. First, a commitment has been made between the coach and client to work together. This is based on the premise that the coach is confident that the client has sufficient commitment to deliver value through sustainable change and the client believes that the coach has the necessary competence to help them. Second, they will have started to develop some trust and rapport. This is unlikely to be fully established, but there will be sufficient strength in the relationship to begin the investigative journey.

Enter the Client stage

At its heart the essence of the Client stage is about two things: understand the person and understand their picture. The coach really does need to get a good feel for the individual's operating patterns, i.e. how they think, feel and behave, both in relation to the topic they want to be coached on and how they manage their normal daily activities. Second, the coach needs to pull the whole picture out from the client about the chosen topic. The key here is to assume that the client:

- has not really thought through the coaching topic and will need help to draw a rich picture;
- is possibly looking at the wrong topic anyway.

Although some people may find the second thought somewhat presumptuous or arrogant, every time I run a Collaborative Coaching course something in the order of 80 per cent of the people change the coaching topic they bring to the event. This is because they realize that the thing they want help on is deeper or different from that which they believe to be the problem. This is where the two models covered in this section can really help. The 3D model helps the coach and client develop a deep understanding of the real person – something that in many cases the client has never had a chance to take time out to understand. Once the person is understood, the next task is to understand the picture, to develop a shared appreciation of their situation and then define what good looks like.

The 3D me

All dimensions are critical dimensions, otherwise why are they there?

Russ Zandbergen

A human being is a complex system involving the interaction of action, emotions and thoughts. These three core dimensions (Figure 6.1) are described in this model as follows:

- The Heart – affective or feeling-based factors.
- The Head – cognitive or what people are thinking or saying to themselves.
- The Hand – behavioural or physiological factors.

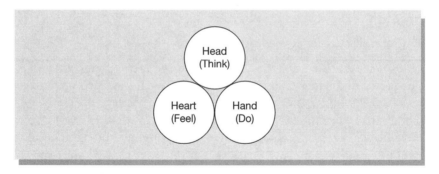

Figure 6.1   3D model

This model is not new or unique. It is the basic psychological view of man that goes back to the Greeks and probably the Egyptians. It views man as composed of three interdependent processes. All interact and no one part can change without the other parts also changing. Becoming emotionally anxious prior to presenting to a large audience might trigger panic thoughts of 'It will all go wrong.' This in turn leads to moist palms and shaky hands. The shaky hands create thoughts of 'Everyone will see my hands tremble when I put the slide up', which creates further anxiety. So the ever-decreasing spiral can be seen to bounce between the three dimensions.

These three dimensions are based on ideas from a particular group of people (Figure 6.2). The heart dimension draws upon the work of Daniel Goleman and his views of emotional intelligence. It also draws upon the work of J.A. Russell's Circumflex model of affect. The Head dimension draws upon the school of cognitive behaviour therapy and the work of Dr Albert Ellis and Aaron T. Beck. The Hand dimension draws upon the ideas of behavioural modification and is influenced by the theories of a group of people. However, there are two dominant players – Ivan Pavlov's view on classical conditioning and B.F. Skinner's operant conditioning.

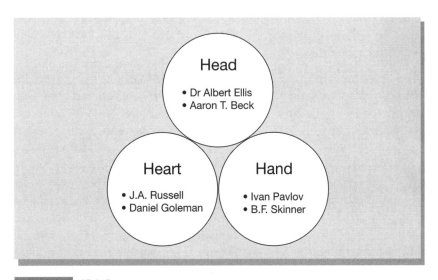

Figure 6.2   3D influencers

The aim in pulling together these three diverse groups of ideas is to help develop a more cohesive and congruent coaching framework – one that takes into account the whole person and not just particular emotional, logical or behavioural factors.

Affective dimension – Heart

It is clear, however, that, without the preferences reflected by positive and negative affect, our experiences would be a neutral gray. We would care no more what happens to us or what we do with our time than does a computer.

C. Daniel Batson, Laura L. Shaw and Kathryn C. Oleson

As you read this page, pause for a second and reflect on what you are feeling. Are you relaxed and almost serene because you have taken the day off and ignored all the washing-up and jobs to be done around the house? Are you slightly anxious because the train is delayed and you are worried that you might be late to the office for the third day running? Are you buzzing because the envelope arrived this morning with the result for the exams you took recently? Or are you somewhat wistful or low because it is the anniversary of a time when something sad happened in your life? You may not be overtly conscious of these feelings, but they are there and their presence will clearly impact on how you read this book and any judgements you form about the ideas.

This is because the heart is the guiding force that helps you make life choices. In his book *Emotional Intelligence*,[1] Daniel Goleman talks about the 'inner rudder', the ability to make intuitive decisions based on subjective hunches or gut feelings. This rudder guides who we are, where we are heading and what course we can take. The powerful thing is that this rudder has an almost instinctive ability. In an unknown situation like a new bar, it can save us from danger as we automatically sense if trouble is brewing and make our exit; it can almost magically warn us that someone is not all they profess to be; or it helps the comic tune into the audience and identify which jokes work and which are likely to bomb. This inner rudder is what saved early humans on the savannah as they made instant fight/flight decisions when faced with unknown or dangerous prey.

> **The heart is the guiding force that helps you make life choices.**

However, this innate and deep guiding force can act to our detriment. It is the untamed power that causes the normally laid-back driver to turn into a raging monster at the traffic lights when he has been cut up by the motorbike rider weaving between traffic; it is the excitement that flashes on our face when the horrible boss announces that she is leaving; it is the black cloud that comes over the person made redundant who can't seem to get themselves out of bed to face yet another interview; or it is the lethargic

1 Goleman, Daniel (1996) *Emotional Intelligence*, Bloomsbury.

feeling that kicks in on a Sunday morning, even when we should be up doing the list of jobs that has been left out by our partner. These emotions have an almost absolute force and direction that little can seem to tame. Just think about that moment when you have been waiting to get through a traffic jam and the fifth person in a row cuts into the queue. The emotional force that can surface is so powerful that it seems almost irresistible. It takes extraordinary effort not to drive into the offending car.

From a coaching perspective, a key part of the coach's value is to help the client understand their emotions and how they act as a personal rudder, driving what they think and do. We have all been in the situation of rationally thinking through what we will say or do when faced with a particular event, only to find that when push comes to shove, the fight/flight mechanism kicks in and our response actually has little to do with the planned behaviour. It is at this point that the emotional rudder has taken hold and directed what we are thinking and doing. Typical emotions that the coach and client need to deal with include:

■ Anxiety	■ Happiness
■ Anger	■ Hope
■ Disgust	■ Hate
■ Depression	■ Love
■ Excitement	■ Pride
■ Fear	■ Rage
■ Guilt	■ Surprise

The coach's role is to help the client momentarily step outside themselves and begin to analyze these emotions from a more objective perspective – to understand how their emotions change; what causes them to change; what impact they have on their life; and what impact they have on the topic they are being coached on. Only by understanding the nature and impact of their emotions will the client be able to manage out those feelings that are not helping deliver their desired outcome.

e-Map

As we consider how to help the client map their emotional state, there is an interesting conundrum. We need the mapping process to be very simple to understand so that it does not become too complex or difficult for the client to use. If the runner wants to map their emotions while preparing for a marathon, they don't want to have to lug around a folder just to remember how to use the model. It needs to be highly accessible and practical so as to facilitate instant use. However, the idea of mapping our emotions is so complex as to be almost impossible. Just think about the sheer range and variance in your emotions, even since you got up today. The breadth and depth of emotional state that you have experienced may seem too difficult to map and manage.

However, while it may not be practical to map all the elements involved in an emotional response, it is possible to select two key parameters. By using these it is feasible to map a set of emotional dynamics that indicates the nature of the affective state the client is experiencing. To do this we can help the client determine:

- what impact the emotions have (pleasant or unpleasant);
- what the level of intensity or energy might be (high or low).

By understanding these two parameters the coach is able to help the client both deal with the emotion and where necessary take action to move between different emotional states. For example, where a client may find they get anxious before presenting to a management board, by being aware of the type and intensity of the emotional state they can train themselves to migrate from a stressed position to one where they can harness the anxiety and turn it into a form of excitement or stimulation.

James Russell researched the idea of affective states and used these two baselines of energy level and impact to construct an emotional map.[2] This idea has been expanded to develop an emotional model that describes four discrete emotional states (Figure 6.3). These four states are used to help the coach and client develop a shared understanding of the emotional forces that impact on the client's ability to deliver sustainable change.

2 Russell, J.A. (1980) 'A circumflex model of affect', *Journal of Personality and Social Psychology, 39*, 1161–78.

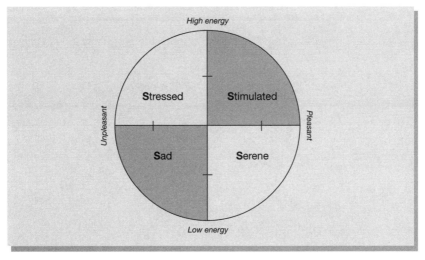

Figure 6.3 e-Map

The important thing to appreciate with the e-Map is not the map itself, but the fact that it offers both the coach and the client a rapid and simple way in which to describe how they feel (Figure 6.4). There are over two thousand words in English used to express emotion. Imagine the difficulty that the client and coach will have in trying to define the emotion for themselves and then finding a way to communicate that. However, by creating a shared map it becomes easier to describe the current emotion and the one that is needed to effect a sustainable solution.

Once expressed it makes sense to discover ways in which to move to an emotional state that might be more fit for the outcome the client wishes to achieve. For example, imagine a client who always fails interviews. Their belief (and evidence backed up by board feedback) is that they are often the preferred candidate, but once in front of the interview panel they begin to lose control, sweat and don't appear to have clarity of thought. By working with the e-Map, the coach can train the client to use the model as a dynamic measurement tool. So the coach might prepare a card with the e-Map on it. The client then begins to use the chart a few days or hours before the interview, tracking their emotional state over time. At any point where they might begin to drift into the Stressed quadrant they can kick in a range of pre-prepared strategies. This might be to call the coach or a colleague to help them dissolve any surfacing fears; to listen to music that calms them; or simply to use a set of personal mantras or anchoring techniques that help migrate them back into the serene or stimulated state.

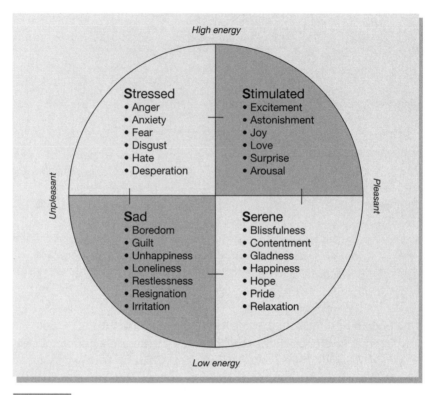

Figure 6.4   e-Map feelings

Often stress or fear is caused by a sense of isolation or uncertainty. The e-Map can help take away some of the emotional uncertainty by helping the client to say, 'Ok, I am currently in the Stressed or Sad quadrant, but I was in the Serene or Stimulated quadrant two hours ago.' The simple fact of knowing the current anxious state is transitory and under the client's control can be enough in itself to ease the pain and facilitate migration to a desired position.

> **Often stress or fear is caused by a sense of isolation or**

Emotional track and trace

This implies that the client must learn to track and trace the movement in their emotional state over time. By making such a map they will be able to understand how their emotions have varied, what the impact of the variance was on personal performance, and what triggers may have pushed them from one state into another. By using such a mapping process it becomes possible for the coach and client to consider alternative strategies that allow the client either to bypass the trigger or to eliminate it altogether.

Consider, for example, the e-Map shown in Figure 6.5, which traces the journey I used to follow when running a new training programme. On a Sunday night I would be relaxing and watching TV and the course might be the last thing on my mind (A). As the evening moves on I begin to think about the course and then get excited about working with a new group of people (B). After that I go to bed, wake up in the morning still in a relaxed state (C). Driving towards the training centre I begin to get excited again (D). However, as I drive up to the centre panic begins to set in as I worry about what I may have forgotten to pack (E). This stress increases (F) but then moves into a stimulated state as I remember that everything is packed and that I will not have any problems. As the course starts, things go well and I really enjoy the session (G) and this carries on until the close. At the end of the course, once the review forms have been handed in, I go into a real dip (H). This is triggered because I anticipated poor reviews. Finally, after the drive home (and Dave Chitty, my colleague, calling to calm me down), I drift into a more related state (I) and the cycle is complete.

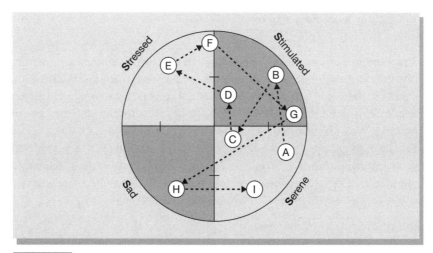

Figure 6.5 e-Map track and trace

The lessons I learned from this were first to try to avoid the slip into the stressed state (point E) by ensuring that all the course material was prepared and checked by colleagues. And second, that talking about my feelings after the course helps me to avoid the Sad shift (point H) on the model. This would produce the map in Figure 6.6, thus beginning to erase some of the stress and sad points that were counterproductive states in the running of a training course. Dave learned this early on with me, as he knew that I would go into a freefall of anxiety, so he would wait for me to call and just let me dump my feelings. Once these were out I could drift into the Serene quadrant and just relax.

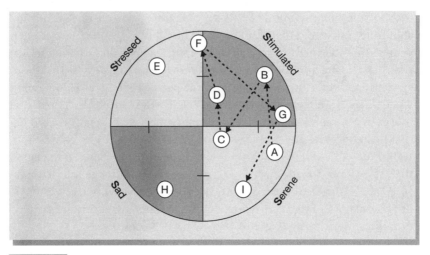

Figure 6.6   **Modified e-Map track and trace**

The interesting thing is that Dave's role as a coach was not to force me from one state to another because the coach has no power to do this. What he did was to surface it as an issue and help me to guide through a process that would work for me. Even clearer is that he did this through the use of humour. When running courses he would jokingly talk about my black hole that I would disappear into following the course. Because it was wrapped in good spirit and fun it allowed the issue to be raised in a non-threatening manner. This in turn allowed us to talk about it and for me to share what he could do that would help me move beyond the low levels.

Hence, the coach's role is to teach the e-Map model to the client, teach them how to map their emotional state and then track it over time. The power of the track and trace approach is that it allows the client to undertake a deep and rigorous analysis in between sessions with the coach and then provides exceptional data that will help the client and coach to fully explore the emotional journey taken in relation to the coaching topic. Once the typical journey is mapped, the coach and client can begin to map what the journey should look like to deliver a sustainable outcome.

Cognitive dimension – Head

As you read this page, stop and think about what you are thinking. What is that little inner voice saying about you, the book and your interpretation of the content? Are you agreeing with the ideas and thinking about how to apply them? Do you have negative views because you have heard the ideas before and can't see anything new in the book? Or do you think that the ideas are too complex and that coaching is an instinctive thing that doesn't really benefit from the use of models and theories? You may not be overtly conscious of these thoughts, but they exist and their presence will clearly impact on how you read this book, the judgements you form, and any consequential actions you take.

❝ Clients usually do not understand the negative effects of their own thoughts. ❞

However, from a coaching perspective, it is the irrational negative assumptions and beliefs that often need to be considered because they act as a brake on the human potential. Clients usually do not understand the negative effects of their own thoughts. Hence the coach must help surface and expose what impact the thought patterns have on their behaviour. To help do this the coach needs to understand the cognitive structures that underpin how people make sense of the world.

We can develop a symbolic representation of our cognitive structures using three levels: Absolutes, Assumptions and Autopilot (Figure 6.7). These three layers are important because they have a direct bearing on the client and in particular what they say and do. The absolute beliefs act as the foundation stone in someone's life, directing both what they do and say but also how they interpret things that others say. The assumptions drive how judgements are formed and decisions are taken because they offer the equations of life, such that when something happens, this will be my response. And the autopilot is the little inner voice – the thing that has immediate impact on what you think, do and say.

If the coach and client want to get to the root of the issue and not simply address the surface symptoms, time needs to be set aside to map and explore (as a minimum) the client's autopilot (or inner voice) routine, and ideally some of the core assumptions they follow. It is clearly beneficial to climb inside some of the absolutes, but in reality these will often take longer to address and may well be the domain of the therapist as opposed to the coach. The danger with dealing in the absolute area is that it can surface all sorts of unintended issues and the coach must ethically have the confidence and competence to be able to help the client deal with these if they surface.

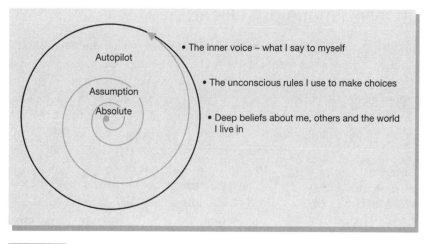

Autopilot

Assumption

Absolute

• The inner voice – what I say to myself

• The unconscious rules I use to make choices

• Deep beliefs about me, others and the world I live in

Figure 6.7   Head maps

Autopilot

A key principle in the Collaborative Coaching framework is that external events do not cause people to act or feel in a certain way. The spider cannot make me scared and the sight of blood cannot make me feel ill – this is my chosen response to the extrinsic trigger. So it is people's interpretation of the external trigger that causes them to act in a certain way. Imagine how two people can see the same film, eat the same meal or date the same person but their chosen responses and perceived experiences will be fundamentally different.

The client often forms this interpretation automatically, without any conscious effort. Like the autopilot on a plane, the pilot and crew can sit back and operate on the assumption that a computer is taking all the most appropriate choices for them. In the same way we all have an autopilot mode, where we let pre-programmed responses to external triggers kick into place without consciously challenging what is happening. However, in the same way that the professional pilot will always keep a watchful eye on the autopilot to ensure it is not making erroneous decisions, we all need to keep a watchful eye on the thought patterns used to make what appear to be simple choices and actions. These can be seen in the constant flow of thoughts, ideas, beliefs and dialogue that takes place in the background while we are managing life. As an example, while reading this book you have been saying things to yourself: points you agree with, disagree with, thoughts about things you can and can't do in relation to the suggestions in the book. That is your autopilot – the guiding voices that drive how you feel and behave.

The coach needs to help the client understand, interpret and in some cases modify these thoughts. This is because some will be positive and help the client to achieve their desired outcome, but some will be counterproductive and act as a barrier to achieving the outcome. Importantly these thoughts are not bad thoughts as such, they are natural cognitive processes that we all have, and the challenge for the coach is to help the client understand those that aid their journey and those that inhibit it. They can look like:

▓ 'That girl is really good-looking – she won't want to speak to me.'

▓ 'I don't think the manager will give me a good review.'

▓ 'I can't do this.'

▓ 'What the hell – I will have another drink as a treat.'

▓ 'I will never get this job done in time – I have too much to do.'

The coach must learn how to help the client map their thoughts. Once mapped, they need to differentiate between those autopilot routines that are helping and those that are disabling the journey.

Assumptions

This level can be seen as the attitudes, rules and hypotheses that we use to create the automatic thoughts. They tend to consist of rules and regulations that help us get through life. These underlying conditional assumptions or rules are an integral part of who we are and what we do on a minute-by-minute basis. They form our personal principles, ideas and viewpoints that we expound when watching TV or conversing with colleagues in a bar.

Some rules and assumptions are positive and helpful: however, others are destructive and can increase the tendency to see the world in a negative way. These rules have a number of characteristics – they can apply across a range of domains, are learned through association with others, often from a young age, can be linked to cultural forces that surround the individual, and are often very fixed in place and hard to change. There are two categories of assumptions:

1 Fundamental rigid assumptions which are conditional beliefs often seen as 'if . . . then' statements.

2 Rules or drivers, which can be heard as 'should' and 'must' statements. These indicate what is right and wrong and how we expect the world to operate when it follows our rules.

Typical examples of cognitive assumptions might be:

- Things must be OK at home before I can take any risks at work.
- It is important to always make the right decision.
- It is terrible to be inadequate.
- If I work extra hours and please the boss then things are OK.
- I need to be best at everything I do.

In listening to the client you can begin to hear many of these assumptions surface. However, sitting underneath these rules is a set of deep belief systems that are their absolutes. These are the embedded maps through which the client will filter all incoming data.

Absolutes

The idea that 'we know more than we can say' lies at the heart of the Head dimension. Our life experiences lay down the framework for a series of tacit beliefs about the way the world works. For example, a child who is deprived at an early age may develop an unspoken rule that 'I must fight for everything I get.' A child who is rejected by his parents may develop a rule that 'I'm unlovable'. These are examples of the core cognitive maps. However, the very fact that they were developed early, often before language development, means they may not be easily identified.

These deep beliefs are the bedrock of the thinking system. They form the foundations of who we are, what we believe about others and our generalized thoughts about the world. They are absolute truths that the individual applies to the whole world and are generally inflexible and resistant to change.

Negative absolutes are distorted opinions, based on self-perception. They are key in shaping our view of life and impact across everything we do. The important thing about these absolutes is that they don't just impact on how we behave in the world – they also disturb and distort the incoming information to fit into the existing set of absolutes. Because of this we filter all incoming data through a set of biased filters. Ideas and thoughts that align with the current worldview are accepted, but data that does not fit the map is rejected as an untruth.

❝Data that does not fit the map is rejected as an untruth.❞

Personally I often wonder just how I have managed to get my books published. As a consequence when I look at the reviews on Amazon, I ignore any positive ones and actively seek out the negative ones thus reaffirming the deep belief that I am lucky to be doing this. A further example of this deep belief is the fact that I hate signing books – not because I am not proud of the work, but because I have a sense of not being worthy and on a par with the authors whose signature means something.

Absolutes might take the form of:

▥ The world is not a nice place.

▥ All people from sales are corrupt.

▥ Nobody can be trusted.

▥ I must worry about things that could be dangerous, unpleasant or frightening – otherwise they might happen.

▥ Every problem should have an ideal solution – and it's intolerable when one can't be found.

Very often people are not aware of their absolutes – they just exist and are used as a guide to drive our choice-making processes. These beliefs might be things like 'always win' or 'life sucks'. These deep and rigid beliefs can cause us to feel stressed because our views leave no room for variety in how we see the world. The coach's role is often to help the client recognize and accept that the client's inflexible, rigid views are the reason they get stressed, can't perform on the track or fail to get promoted at work. Only by helping the client to look inside and see these deep and absolute beliefs can they start to challenge and change those that are limiting the client's ability to progress.

The coach has a difficult job because they must be able to identify all the possible assumptions just by listening to the client language, as seen in Figure 6.7. This is no easy task and one that can take many years of practice. But when developed it is a key tool in the coach's armoury.

Just by asking the client how things are and getting responses like 'I just don't seem to be able to get promoted – maybe I don't deserve it' can open up a floodgate of deep reasons why the client is actually 'choosing' to fail their interviews. Not knowingly, but at a deep level, because somewhere they have picked up an absolute about the world and their role in it which has in turn created an assumption about themselves.

The danger is that if the coach doesn't pick up on the embedded issues in this type of client statement, they might fall into the trap of agreeing with the client suggestion that they should undertake a three-year management degree course to help gain promotion. The trouble is that if the embedded assumptions or autopilots are not resolved, the client will take a degree course and still not get promoted. The net result is that they might then believe that doing a Masters degree programme is the answer. This can carry on ad infinitum, whereas the real issue is that the client has deep baggage about themselves and they are applying brakes in the form of limiting beliefs that can (with work) be released.

Common auto-maps

The combination of the autopilot, assumptions and absolutes can result in a series of negative autopilot patterns that can prevent the client from making any real headway. In reality most negative patterns are quite generic and will be seen to fit into a number of common routines. A few of the more common ones include the following:

- **Absotruths** – make sweeping conclusion about a minor situation and turn it into an absolute truth. This can include creating false labels for self and others – for example, 'Because I didn't pass the interview I am crap and will never get a new job.' Or, 'Because the person didn't acknowledge my hello in the corridor, that means they don't like me.'

- **Be the best** – set personal standards that are far beyond the plausible levels that can be met by most people. This is referred to as 'musturbation' as it highlights the way people use unconditional shoulds and musts in the belief that specific things must happen for them to be whole. They must be loved, they should achieve certain goals and they must do well in all things.

- **Choice capping** – see only two options when there are many possible actions that can be taken. This can be seen at the solution stage of the coaching session, when the client swears blind that they have only two possible solutions and really believe that they have no other options available.

- **Discounting the positives** – choose to turn down the positive and turn up the negative thoughts and outcomes. In many cases a client will absolutely refuse to listen to positive feedback even when it is thrust in their face.

- **Emotional overload** – let emotions rule what seems to be logical choice.

- **Fluke** – believe that one day the truth will out and people will find out that they are really no good. This is a common occurrence – especially when people are promoted rapidly within an organization and are not convinced that it is warranted.

▦ **Guessing game** – believe that you can see into the unknown. This might be an ability to look into the future and predict what will happen or to look into other people's minds and know what they are thinking.

The more the coach can help a client identify, understand and address these negative autopilots (NAPs), the greater is the chance they will help deliver sustainable value. This is where the whole emphasis of the Collaborative Coaching framework is education based. It is not sufficient to help the client see and deal with a particular negative autopilot – the goal is to train them so they can catch and manage future NAPs. Only by making this type of educational intervention can the coach truly walk away at the end of the change process feeling and knowing that they have delivered sustainable value.

Challenging the client's map

Clearly, the ability to help the client challenge any NAPs can be quite a specialized skill that needs a great deal of practice and care. When attempting to modify such underlying belief systems there are a few possible guidelines.

1 Try not to criticize the client's thoughts as wrong. It is more a case of encouraging the client to consider what benefit the thought pattern offers and how it might help achieve the desired outcome. So a non-judgemental Socratic approach might be taken where the goal is to help the client explore what they know rather than appearing critical in what to them is a natural and normal way of viewing the world. This would be akin to someone saying to me that my belief about the type of music I like is wrong. They might have a view on that, but their viewpoint will do little to help encourage me to search out other types of music.

2 Try to frame feedback using the words and (where possible) similar intonation to that used by the client. We all receive language and then play it back with a slight degree of distortion. This might be in a rephrasing of a particular word or by placing emphasis on a different part of the sentence. What might appear to be a minor change to the coach can be a major shift in the client's ears and can cause them to misunderstand or possibly withdraw from the coaching process.

3   Try not to open a can of worms by seeking to 'out' all the apparent NAPs. The goal is to surface and deal with those that limit the client's ability to move forward, not undergo a massive therapeutic session. Although you might hear lots of potential thought patterns that limit their ability to be who they are and what they want to be, the coach has no divine right to intervene in the client's life to 'make it better'. The coaching contract should be clear as to where the coach is providing support and this should be the only area of concern.

4   Never forget that only the client can choose to change an autopilot or assumption. You cannot change it for them. You cannot put your hand inside their head and erase memories, reframe history or rebuild a particular thought pattern. Hence if the client really doesn't want to change a NAP, that must be their choice. All the coach can do is to help give them the chance to be aware of the NAP and its impact.

5   Try to make sure that the process of changing NAP is one of 'running to' rather than 'running from'. Don't get the client to a position where they don't like their thought patterns and just want to discard them. Instead help them see that an alternative way of thinking will offer benefits and as such there is a pull into another state. Often the running from process can leave residual guilt and a shadow desire to go back to that way of thinking. To help with this process try to offer many alternatives for them to select from. By creating a positive array of alternative views the client can gain great benefit just from recognizing that there are other ways to view the world and that their current one can be modified.

6   All ways of thinking can offer value, it just depends on context. Just because you don't understand why someone constantly limits themselves, for them it serves a valuable purpose, otherwise they wouldn't do it. So when helping them to reflect on their thoughts, try to help them think about what positive aspects that thought pattern serves and what the impact will be of giving it up. One important thing with this is that what you as the coach might view as a NAP might well be a positive autopilot for them. Don't make arbitrary judgements about the associated value of a thought pattern until you have tested what benefit the client derives from the activity.

7   It can help to encourage the client to rate the strength of the NAP. By understanding the degree of strength behind a particular thought pattern it helps you as a coach to make certain choices about the wisdom of seeking to modify the pattern, the amount of energy that

will be necessary to effect a change and the type of intervention that might be necessary to help effect a sustainable change.

The coach might employ a range of questions that can challenge the client to listen to what they are thinking. As a coach you might use questions like:

- What is the evidence for this idea?
- What evidence supports it?
- What evidence is there that counteracts the idea?
- Is there an alternative explanation?
- What is the worst that could happen and how would you deal with it?
- What is the best that could happen?
- What will probably happen?
- What value does having this thought have on achieving your goal?
- How would others view what you are describing?
- What other thoughts might help achieve your outcome?
- What advice would you offer a friend who had the same thoughts?

The Head dimension in summary

The ideas covered in the Head section of the 3D model barely touch the surface of the cognitive aspects of coaching. For more rigour and depth about this subject you should seek out the work of Albert Ellis and Aaron T. Beck, who are often viewed as the founding fathers of the school of cognitive behaviour therapy. However, for the mainstream coach, the ideas introduced here provide a good outline of what need to be considered and mapped early on in the coaching assignment.

By recognizing that the client will have three levels of thought operating in any coaching process, the coach can form an opinion on how to help and, maybe more importantly, whether they can really help. In some cases you can't because the client doesn't really want to or isn't prepared to let go of destructive NAPs. The coach can only inform, challenge and educate – they cannot make the client change their autopilots.

❝ The coach can only inform, challenge and educate. ❞

Behavioural dimension – Hand

As you read this page, stop and think about what you are doing. What little habits do you have without realizing it? (Mine is tapping.) When coaching, what do you do without thinking (like how you greet someone) and what behaviours have you developed that help make things happen (like the use of friendly touching to build rapport)? You may not be overtly conscious of these behaviours or habits, but they exist and their presence will clearly impact on how you coach others.

The last of the three dimensions to be considered are the physical or behavioural aspects. With this we seek to understand why clients do what they do. For example, when coaching someone who wants to give up smoking but finds it difficult as they keep reverting, one of the aspects to look at may be the behavioural action they take at the point when the habits kick in again. Just why do people do what they do? Is it because they think it is the right thing? Is it because they get an emotional need? Or is it simply because of a habit – where something instinctive takes over before they even have a chance to think about what is happening? Maybe their friend offers a cigarette – without thinking they take one and light up. It can help the coaching process to explore what happens at that moment and consider what conditional reflex processes were taking place that triggered the response.

This dimension is explored using the school of behaviourism. This is a theory of learning that focuses on observable behaviours and tends to discount emotional and mental activities. Behaviour theorists define learning as simply the acquisition of new behaviour.

There are two different ways of looking at why we do what we do (Figure 6.8):

1 **Reactive** or **classical conditioning** occurs when there is a natural response to an extrinsic stimulus.

2 **Proactive** or **operant conditioning** occurs when reward or reinforcement creates behaviour and as a consequence the behaviour becomes more probable in the future.

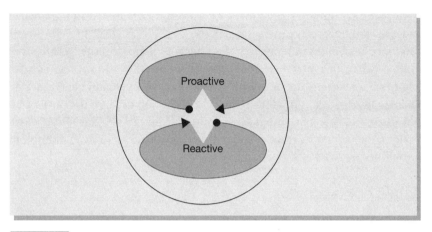

Figure 6.8   Proactive and reactive conditioning

Reactive conditioning

In reactive conditioning people habitually do something in response to external stimuli. This was made famous by Pavlov's experiments with dogs. Pavlov presented dogs with food and measured their salivary response (how much they drooled). He then began to ring a bell just before presenting the food. After a while, the dogs began to salivate at the sound of the bell. They learned to associate the sound of the bell with the presentation of the food. As far as their immediate physiological responses were concerned, the sound of the bell became equivalent to the presentation of the food.

This can be seen in the workplace as people change the web page when they hear the boss walking down the aisle or slow down for a comfort break at the smell of coffee brewing. Hence reactive conditioning is often a habit that develops over time, but people cannot always explain why it has developed – it just has.

Stimuli that people react to automatically are called *primary* or *unconditioned stimuli*. They include food, pain, and other 'hardwired' or 'instinctive' stimuli. Stimuli that people react to only after learning about them are called *secondary* or *conditioned stimuli*. In Pavlov's experiment, the sound of the bell meant nothing to the dogs at first. After its sound was associated with the presentation of food, it became a conditioned stimulus. This can be seen as new people join a work team and begin to learn the associated cues and triggers of the other team members.

The pairing of stimuli shapes many of our behaviours. How can the smell of a rich scent, a certain tune, a specific day of the year result in quite strong feelings? It's not that the smell or the song are the cause of the emotion, but rather what that smell or song has been paired with . . . perhaps an emotional relationship, or the day you went to see a certain band play. We make these associations all the time and often don't realize the power that these connections or pairings have on us. But, in fact, we have been classically conditioned to react without thinking about or understanding our reaction.

Proactive conditioning

This is a form of learning in which we determine how specific behaviours lead to specific consequences. It can be thought of as 'learning by consequences'. So we develop habits based on anticipated responses.

The classic study of proactive or operant conditioning involves a cat which is placed in a box with only one way out; a specific area of the box has to be pressed in order for the door to open. In its attempt to escape, the cat triggers the area of the box and the door opens, enabling the cat to escape. Once placed in the box again, the cat will naturally try to remember what it did to escape the previous time and will once again find the area to press. It has learned, through natural consequences, how to gain freedom.

We all learn this way in everyday life. Whenever a mistake is made we hopefully remember what happened and do things differently when it comes along again. In that sense, you've learned to act differently based on the natural consequences of your previous actions. The same holds true for positive actions. If something you did results in a positive outcome, you are likely to do that same activity again.

Helping the client change what they 'do'

The coach is often there to help the client understand why they do what they do, to question when they exhibit a specific behaviour – do they do this because they consciously believe it is the optimum behaviour, or do they do it because that is what they have always done?

If the behaviour is sub-optimal or unwanted, the coach can then help the client appreciate whether the behaviour has come about as a result of reactive or proactive conditioning. Do they do what they do because others do it and it is just the accepted thing? Or do they actively manage it because it offers a payback? Does the client say they want to be more assertive at work but habitually fail to speak loudly to assert themselves? Is it because they have adopted the norm for the environment, i.e. no one else raises their voice against certain people? Or is it because by not raising their voices they do not have to stand out in the crowd and face the possible consequences in being more visible to their colleagues?

A key part of the coach's role is to offer feedback and observations to the client on behaviours they exhibit and in part on ones that they were not aware of. Maybe the client does things, says

> **ĠĠ A key part of the coach's role is to offer feedback and observations. ĠĠ**

things or behaves in a certain way that has significant impact on their desired goal but they fail to realize quite how detrimental it is. Because it is a conditioned behaviour and the client regards it as 'normal', they will possibly not be aware of its existence. By helping the client to be cognisant of their behaviour and its impact, the coach can help bring about a real and sustainable change for the client.

Managing the 3D model

In bringing the three dimensions together we can see the resulting 3D model in Figure 6.9. The potential complexity of the client operating system can be observed as we see the different forces that act together to influence how we feel, think and behave.

In considering the 3D model we can begin to trace the underlying patterns that emerge in certain circumstances. For example, in preparing for a presentation I begin to feel 'nervous' – as a result NAPs kick in and I begin to think counterproductive thoughts such as 'I am not prepared for this' which in turn triggers behaviour learned from previous experience where problems were anticipated – namely 'shaking hands'. This pattern can emerge over a period of seconds or it might take hours. Much of the coach's work is to help the client map the pattern as it occurs and develop a strategy to break the habit.

Another example might be the golfer about to tee off at the first hole who 'mis-strokes'. The physical error triggers sudden anxiousness, especially because he doesn't want to look stupid in front of his friends. This anxiety then triggers negative autopilot thoughts like 'Oh no, I am going to blow the rest of the day now.' The interesting thing is that the golfer may drop into a negative spiral where the NAPs cause him to perform poorly on the next three holes, which in turn creates more anxiety. The next result is that

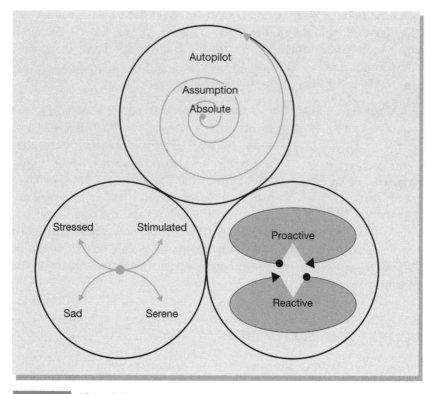

Figure 6.9   3D model

he slams the club on the floor, curses and decides to give up golf for ever. This spiral pattern can be seen in Figure 6.10.

This is a spiral decent process that can inflict pain on so many people. Look at top sportsmen in the pre-match interview. I remember one who when talking about the next tournament was already using words like 'might win' and 'hope', and guess what – he lost. The deep inner descent down the spiral meant that he was preparing himself for the worst. Now, clearly, telling yourself that you will doesn't guarantee that you will – but it does give you more of a fighting chance, whereas telling yourself you will not succeed offers a pretty good bet that you will fail.

The coach's role is to listen carefully when the client describes themselves and their topic, then to figure out whether the client is in a spiral and if so, how deep they have gone down. With the example of the dieter who can't seem to lose weight, it is easy for the coach to follow a false trail by getting the client to focus on their eating habits and dietary regime, but it may be

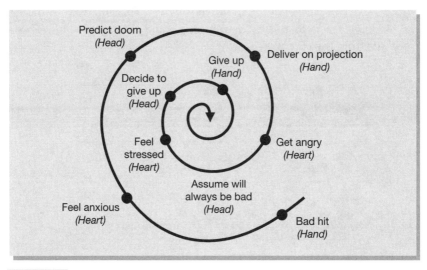

Figure 6.10 3D spiral descent

that the coach needs to climb further down the 3D spiral and look at the moment when the client gave up, map what the person is feeling, thinking and doing at that point, and try to address this rather than the issue of food. It may be that the coaching topic should be on how to learn from mistakes as opposed to how to lose weight. For the golfer in the previous example the coaching might be less on how to improve the hit and more on how not to see a miss-hit as a failure and place a pause button between the Heart and Head, thus preventing the negative autopilots from kicking in.

Pushing the pause button

If the coach can give the client the ability to push the pause button, this is possibly the greatest single intervention they can make in the whole coaching journey. We can see in Figure 6.11 how the different dimensions will drive a response in the other dimension; the danger is when this amplifies in intensity and speed. Think of the parent with a young baby. In the early days when the baby comes home from hospital, the crying might cause some tension, but the parent is able to contain too much anxiety and negative thought. As such they don't overreact by getting upset or shouting at the baby. But over time the parent may lose the ability to control the spiral process (especially if they are a single parent with no help or no one to talk to). After a while the triggers increase in strength and arrive at a quicker rate. The end result is that at the first sign of the baby becoming upset the parent either cries or shouts at the baby. This adds to the problem as the baby reacts to this by getting upset and this in turn provokes a response from the parent.

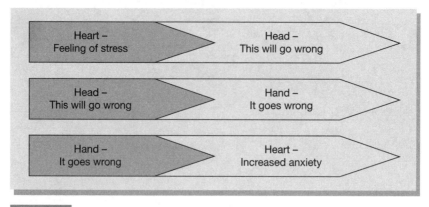

Figure 6.11 Dimension drivers

It might be in this case that the client seeks help because they believe they are not a good parent. The role of the coach is to explore this belief and maybe get the client to focus more on their spiral process and understand the triggers. These can be extrinsic (baby crying, being alone, etc.) or intrinsic (anxiety, stress, etc.). Once they understand these the coach can begin to trace the spiral path the client follows and then help them build in a 'pause point' to prevent the negative loop that they follow, as seen in Figure 6.12.

Other pause buttons might be helping the nervous presenter pause the stammering and fidgety hands by getting them to repeat a mantra over and over again; helping the nervous team member push a pause button when they first enter the office by developing a selection of casual conversation lines; or helping the person with low self-esteem by preparing a card that lists all their great attributes. The only right way to do this is the way that works for the client. The trick is to understand the client well enough to help them track the spiral as it occurs and understand where they can insert a pause and so stop the descent before they spiral out of control.

It is so often people's inability to choose their choice that causes many of the problems that coaches have to deal with. Dieting is often about choosing celery over chocolate; promotion is about saying the right thing rather than getting angry with the boss; and gaining qualifications is about not being put off by the ice and snow.

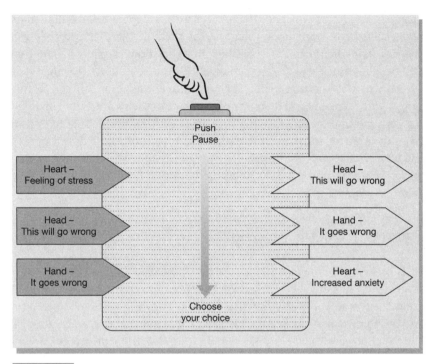

Figure 6.12 Pause button

The coach's role might be seen to follow these steps:

1 Understand to what extent the 'problem' is part of a 3D spiral.

2 Map the spiral process and see how far the client has descended.

3 Try to climb back up the spiral to understand what steps triggered the descent.

4 Help the client understand how resolving the spiral descent may resolve their core problem, even if they don't seem connected.

5 Map in more detail each of the trigger points.

6 Insert a pause point into the process and then allow the client to try out the process to see what happens.

7 Review how successful they have been and work at the process until the client is able to pause at will and make choices that help achieve their perfect picture.

The interesting thing is that of all the steps, when working with a client the hardest part is often step 4. If the client believes that they cannot insert pause points, they will not attempt it. So often people believe that some external force is acting upon them making them do these things. They will believe that when they are upset they 'have' to shout at someone and that this is something they can never change. This can be seen with the road-rage driver who believes that he has no control over the point between feeling angry with someone and then hitting them. The coach's role is to help them understand that just because they get upset with someone it doesn't mean they have to stop for an argument. If they can accept the principle that they do have choice, and that this choice extends to a micro level sitting between what they feel, think and do, then the hard part of their rehabilitation is almost complete.

The PAUSE point model

It is very easy for me to offer these ideas in the cold light of day and say if you just do this then everything will be OK. However, I know only too well that there is a world of difference between knowing what to do to fix a problem and actually doing it. The dieter will know that they must not pick up the chocolate: the question is, will they know it before or after the event? In many (if not most) cases the coach will be dealing with a client who has some form of addictive behaviour. This may not be full-on addiction in the sense of drugs, drink or debt, but addictive in the sense that the client has developed really strong comfort patterns around a behaviour and so finds it difficult to let go.

Only when the argument is over do the couple think to push the pause button, go for a walk and then say sorry. The danger at this point is that the client works on the assumption that they have failed and give up the whole change process and revert to the addictive habit. The coach's role at this point is to help turn the potentially negative outcome into a positive learning point.

The coach can achieve this by helping the client to step back from the pause point and see it from a wider temporal plane. When people are in the pit of confusion, self-doubt and despair, all they tend to see is what is happening now and they forget everything else that has taken place. Talk with the person who has just been made redundant, the middle-aged man whose partner has just walked out or the teenager who has failed their driving test for the third time. All they will see is this huge flashing beacon in front of their eyes

❝ This neon beacon is so bright that it is all they can see. ❞

saying 'YOU HAVE FAILED AND WILL ALWAYS FAIL'. This neon beacon is so bright that it is all they can see.

The coach needs to help them step back from this beacon, turn down the intensity and instead take a broader look at what has happened. They can do this by using the 5-point PAUSE model. Take any coaching topic where the client habitually does something that they later regret. This might be someone dealing with road rage, poor presentations or nerves at interviews. In all these cases there is a common cycle as seen in Figure 6.13.

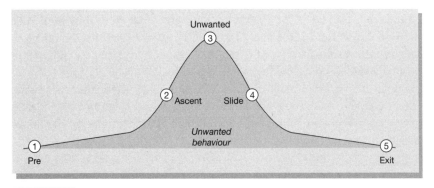

Unwanted

③

② Ascent   Slide ④

Unwanted
behaviour

①

⑤

Pre   Exit

Figure 6.13 PAUSE point model

If we take the road-rage driver, they might be driving down the road without a care in the world and happily listening to the radio (Point 1 – Pre stage). As they approach some roadworks a long queue has built up so they slowly crawl along with everyone else. However, they have been in situations before where people tend to come down alongside the queue and try to cut in at the very end. They remember this and begin to get wound up at the thought of it. They start to look in the side mirror for anyone trying to do this. This begins to raise their emotional anxiety and the NAPs kick in as they are expecting the worst to happen. At this point they have shifted to Point 2 on the model (Ascent). Finally, it happens: along comes the driver who tries to cut in the front. Because our driver is well up the Ascent stage, all it takes is an arrogant look from the other driver and they are at Point 3 – with the unwanted feelings, thoughts and behaviours kicking in. They are out of the car screaming and shouting at the other driver. Luckily the driver manages to speed off and the guy gets back into the car and begins the Slide down the other side of the hump. At Point 4 they might experience a mix of thoughts and feelings. There might be satisfaction because they 'gave them what for' or they might want to return to Point 3 and give chase to sort it out for good. Finally they drive off and begin to calm down and revert to the pre-hump stage. Now at Point 5 (Exit) they might begin to regret what happened and curse themselves for falling into the trap of road anger – something they have been trying to deal with for years.

The coach's role is to help ensure they don't give up and just decide that the problems cannot be resolved. Instead, the coach should help and encourage the client to reflect on what happened and chart the change they experienced over a timeframe. Once charted they can agree at what point the client actually pushed the pause button. The client might agree that they pushed it at Point 5, while although too late to stop the action taking place, at least they pushed it. The coach can then agree what point they would like to push it next time. If the client has deeply embedded habits, it might well be sufficient to aim for a Point 4 pause next time. Hence the coaching might not be about stopping the behaviour but rather about helping the client to manage the pause points. Eventually they should get to the stage where the client is able to push the pause button on the Ascent stage and then ideally at the Pre stage – the moment they feel themselves climbing up the hump (Figure 6.14).

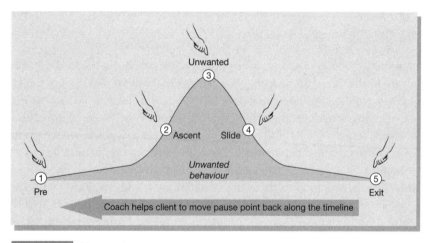

Figure 6.14 Managed pauses

By helping the client understand the five key stages in the PAUSE model, the coach can help them be aware of reversion and understand when the bad habits are creeping in and what they can do about it. No matter what the coaching topic, where the client is trying to change a bad habit into a good one the PAUSE pattern will probably be visible. For example, the presenter who makes a mess and then recognizes why it went wrong or the manager who has chewed someone out when it wasn't really their fault. The more the client is able to learn the PAUSE process, the greater chance they have of managing themselves when faced with addictive forces. Even if the client hits the pause button in the Slide stage and after the negative action has been taken, it doesn't matter, because that is better than hitting the pause button at the Exit stage. By learning to hit at the Slide stage, they will be able to learn to hit the pause button at the Unwanted stage and again with practice will be able to do this with some ease. The PAUSE framework is to help the client appreciate that they can choose their responses and that it is never too late to choose.

It is therefore important to understand that the 3D model considered in this section and seen in Figure 6.1 might look relatively simple but is in fact a more complex process than might be considered at first sight. To this end if you as a coach wish to use this model and some of the derivations outlined in the rest of the book, it is important to spend some time thinking about how it applies to the relationship between you and your client. If possible do further background research using the sources listed earlier, and finally be brave enough to look at your 3D spirals. Only by understanding your descent process can you truly help others understand theirs.

Coaching questions

Key questions might be based around two themes: to understand how each dimension operates and then to delve further to appreciate how these three dimensions interrelate.

3D independent questions

■ What are you feeling at the moment? (Use the e-Map as a template.)

■ Why are you feeling that?

■ Is it a feeling you want to change?

■ What would you like to feel?

■ What are you thinking or saying to yourself?

■ Why do you think you are saying that?

■ What does this mean about you?

■ How are you behaving?

■ Why are you behaving that way and could you do something different?

■ How would you like to behave?

3D interdependent questions

- To what extent are your feelings driving what you are thinking?
- To what extent are your thoughts triggering a certain feeling?
- How are your thoughts impacting on what you are doing?
- How are your feelings influencing what you do?
- In what way are your behaviors influencing your feelings?
- To what extent are your behaviors impacting on what you are thinking?

Pause questions

- At what point did you realize that the choice being made was not right?
- What did you feel when you realized this?
- What were you thinking?
- What did you do?
- What would be the benefit of pushing the pause button before it happens?
- Do you think you might be able to push the pause button before it happens next time?
- At what point might you realistically be able to push the pause button next time?
- What can I do to help you push the button?
- What can you do now to help yourself push the pause button next time?

MPH – paint the picture

Each painting has its own way of evolving . . . When the painting is finished, the subject reveals itself.

William Baziotes

Once the coach understands the client and how the three dimensions (Heart, Head and Hand) are likely to impact, the next stage is to gain an appreciation of the issue they wish to address. In doing this they need to build a rich picture – one that is probably richer and more detailed than the client has considered. The rich picture will have data in nine key areas:

- Meta – The overall outline of the situation.
- Macro – General examples of the issue.
- Micro – Specific information about it.

▦ Past – What has been happening.

▦ Present – What is happening.

▦ Projected – What they want to happen.

▦ Heart – Their feelings about it.

▦ Head – The logic behind it: why it exists.

▦ Hand – The behavioural factors: what they are doing.

Meta	Macro	Micro
Describe in general terms	Give an example	Describe in more detail
Past	**Present**	**Projected**
Looking back...	At present...	In the future...
Heart	**Head**	**Hand**
How do you feel?	Why is this?	What are you doing?

Figure 6.15 MPH model

Although the goal is to get data in all the nine boxes seen in Figure 6.15, the practical aspects tend to be more difficult than this. This is because clients will have a tendency to describe the story using a frame of reference they are comfortable with. So some people will prefer to operate at the concept level (Meta), while others will prefer to describe their issue in detail (Micro); some might need to talk about where they are going (Projected) and others to focus on what is happening now (Present); and some might talk about what they are doing (Hand) but others will seek to describe their feelings (Heart). This preference is a natural process and one that has a major impact on how clients will describe their story in the first instance.

For example, if the client has a preference for 'Meta, Past, Head', they will spend most of the time describing what happened in their background. They will talk about the programme they ran, the strategic benefits it offered, the general background to their problem and where it came from. What you might find difficult to unearth is how they felt about what happened (Heart), what they actually did (Hand), what they are doing now (Present), what they want to do (Projected) or the specific detail of what they do (Micro). Without these other factors you are getting only a small window on their life, and as such it is difficult to help them find a sustainable resolution to their issue.

The coach must learn to recognize when such a bias is emerging in the way that the client is painting their picture and ensure that they can move them into the other domains to get all the necessary information. The power of the MPH framework is designed to help understand what the client is telling you but, more importantly, also what they are not telling you.

> **❝ The power of the MPH framework is designed to help understand what the client is telling you. ❞**

For example, if you have a client who has a 'Meta, Projected, Heart' preference, they will spend all their time exposing where they are going with great passion and verve. What you might get very little of is what has happened (Past) and what they are doing now (Present) about the issue. You may not get any operational example of what needs to happen (Macro) and have little chance of understanding what this change will mean in any detail (Micro). Finally, although they are giving you passion about the change, you may struggle to find the logic behind it (Head) and what they will need to do (Hand).

In this case once the coach has got the Meta, Projected and Heart data, they need to place emphasis on the other six areas. They will need to ask questions like:

- Can you give me some examples of this problem? (Macro)
- Can you give me some specific details about the issue under consideration? (Micro)
- What happened in the past and how did you get to this point? (Past)
- Can you describe what is happening at the moment? (Present)
- How do you feel about this – what are the highs and lows? (Heart)
- Why is this important and what is the rationale behind the problem? (Head)
- What are you doing to help or hinder this issue? (Hand)

One important point here is that the coach has explicitly not attempted to:

- climb inside the client's position to understand what has caused the problem as this comes in the Clarify stage;

- offer a solution or even hinted at things that might help the client (avoid using 'could', 'would' or 'should') as this will come in the Create stage;

- talk about what will need to be 'done' as this will be considered in the Create stage.

The coach is simply trying to start with the blank canvas and paint a rich and detailed picture they can both work with. Once this picture is developed the next stage is to build a clear outcome – what it is the client wants to achieve and in essence to help them create the perfect picture – what good will look like.

The perfect picture

Finally, the MPH framework can help answer the question, 'What does good look like?' At this point it can pay to get the client to relax and describe the future state. Although this sounds simple, very often the client will know what they don't want but have not crystallized what they do want. They are often desperate to get rid of the old ways of being but haven't thought through what they are running towards. This is why the coach needs to help the client really visualize the end point and put a stake in the ground to anchor the future.

This notion of visualization is a common theme in so many areas. The process of creating a picture of the perfect end state and then fixing on this as an outcome is used extensively in sports, in the business market and in therapy relationships. It is often reported that the process of visualization can make a big difference to the coaching journey, primarily because it offers a clear sense of purpose to the process and helps people through the hard times when they are tempted to slip back to the old ways of feeling, thinking, behaving.

By focusing on the projected pattern it is possible to develop a set of 'perfect picture' questions:

- Can you describe in broad terms what will be different when we have finished the journey? (Meta)

- Can you give me some examples of what will be happening when it is complete? (Macro)

■ Can you take one of these examples and talk me through in detail what will be happening when it is complete? (Micro)

■ Can you describe how you will be feeling when it is complete? (Heart)

■ What will you be saying to yourself when the outcome is achieved? (Head)

■ What will you be doing differently when complete? (Hand)

By drawing answers from the client around these and other projected questions the coach and client should develop a clear understanding of what good looks like, as seen in Figure 6.16.

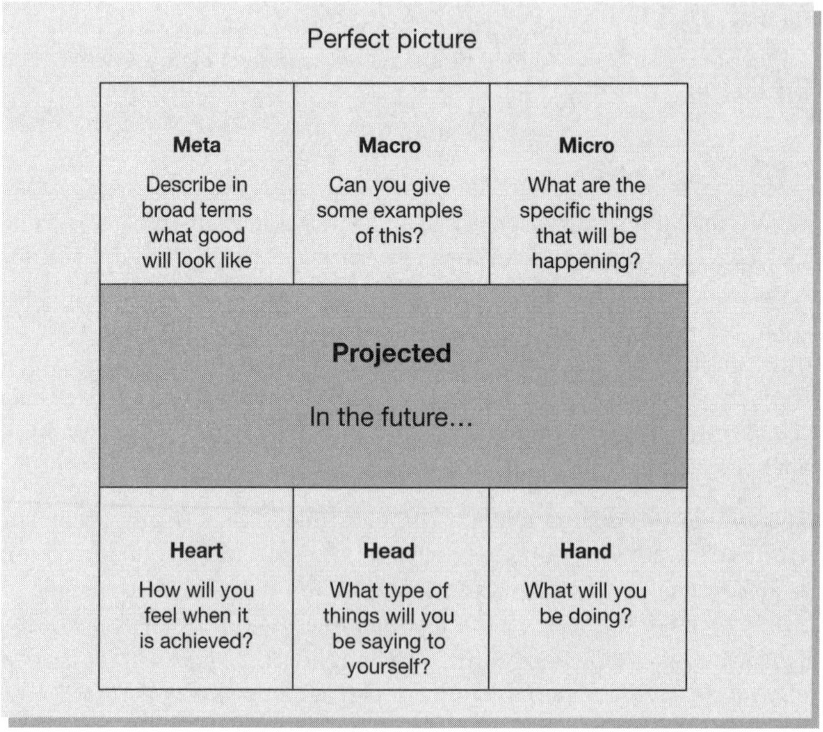

Perfect picture		
Meta Describe in broad terms what good will look like	**Macro** Can you give some examples of this?	**Micro** What are the specific things that will be happening?
Projected In the future...		
Heart How will you feel when it is achieved?	**Head** What type of things will you be saying to yourself?	**Hand** What will you be doing?

Figure 6.16   Perfect picture map

The additional benefit of gathering this type of rich data will be understood when we reach the Confirm and Continue stages of the framework. By getting this type of specific data the coach and client are able to set clear and measurable parameters that help them understand when the client is on target or drifting off target. It also allows the coach to help the client be really clear and sure that they have reached the end goal. For example, someone might be trying to give up smoking and because they haven't smoked for four weeks may believe that the coaching relationship can end. However, if the perfect picture included the need to not just give up smoking but also feel no tension or stress when in the presence of people who smoke, it might be that the perfect picture has not been achieved. It might be that the coaching partnership will need to continue for a while until all elements within the picture have been realized.

Coaching questions

(Meta, Past, Heart) –	What are your feelings about what has been happening?
(Meta, Past, Head) –	Why do you think this occurred?
(Meta, Past, Hand) –	What have you been doing?
(Macro, Past, Heart) –	Pick one aspect of what happened and tell me how you felt about it.
(Macro, Past, Head) –	What were your thoughts on this issue?
(Macro, Past, Hand) –	Give an example of what you were doing at the time.
(Micro, Past, Heart) –	Can you hone down and really help me understand how you felt at that moment?
(Micro, Past, Head) –	What were you specifically saying to yourself then?
(Micro, Past, Hand) –	How did you behave when that specific thing happened – how did you react?
(Meta, Present, Heart) –	How do you feel about the whole thing at the moment?
(Meta, Present, Head) –	What are your general thoughts?
(Meta, Present, Hand) –	What type of things are you doing?
(Macro, Present, Heart) –	Give an example of something that is happening and what your feelings are about it.
(Macro, Present, Head) –	Why did you describe it that way?
(Macro, Present, Hand) –	What are your behaviours associated with this incident?
(Micro, Present, Heart) –	Taking one specific example, describe what is going on inside you. How do you really feel?
(Micro, Present, Head) –	Looking at this moment, what are you saying to yourself?
(Micro, Present, Hand) –	Describe your behaviours in detail.
(Meta, Projected, Heart) –	How would you like to feel in the future?
(Meta, Projected, Head) –	Why is that a good strategy or outcome?

(Meta, Projected, Hand) –   What sort of things will you be doing?

(Macro, Projected, Heart) –   Draw a picture of something happening in the future –
                              how will you feel about it?

(Macro, Projected, Head) –   Why is that a good example?

(Macro, Projected, Hand) –   Give an example of what you will be doing.

(Micro, Projected, Heart) –   Taking one specific moment, what will you be feeling at
                              that moment in time?

(Micro, Projected, Head) –   What will you be saying to yourself?

(Micro, Projected, Hand) –   What will you be doing at that moment in time?

John's journey

At the first meeting Julie explained that she wanted to understand John the person before taking time to understand in more depth the issue he wanted help with. To do this she spent a short time explaining the '3D Me' model.

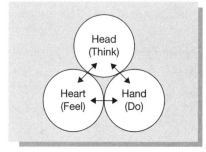

3D me

Because Julie did not delve too deeply into many of the underlying theoretical models John picked up the framework very quickly, and within a short while they were able to really explore John and how he typically operated across the three dimensional areas. To do this Julie asked John to talk about his experiences in dealing with the highs and lows in his life and then they charted the typical responses against the 3D Me model.

John had a tendency to move into the sad quadrant. Although as a relatively docile person he ventured into the Stressed quadrant only when seemingly natural, there were certain triggers that would make him feel quite low and unhappy. This in turn would often lead to periods of stagnation where he would suffer from paralysis from analysis and little would happen.

Often this shift to inactivity was triggered by self-comparison with friends whom he felt were better educated and more well informed than he was about life. He worried about his lack of formal education and this self-doubt always popped into his head in the company of his friends and colleagues.

Julie felt confident that there was sufficient evidence to focus on these as she noticed how John behaved differently in the company of others and that he seemed more at ease with colleagues rather than senior managers.

Once Julie was clear that she had a better measure of John and his dimensional drivers, she wanted to understand John's issue in a lot more depth. She first explained the MPH framework to him and stressed that it was a tool to help draw a picture of the coaching issue. But because it maybe explored ways of looking at the issue from a perspective that he was not used to considering, it might be that she would seem to challenge him in more areas than others.

Meta	Macro	Micro
Describe in general terms	Give an example	Describe in more detail
Past	**Present**	**Projected**
Looking back...	At present...	In the future...
Heart	**Head**	**Hand**
How do you feel?	Why is this?	What are you doing?

MPH

This proved to be the case because John's preferred shape was Meta, Projected, Heart. He gave a wonderfully rich description of the broad idea that he wanted to achieve, but was unable to really explain in detail what would be happening. Because of this Julie pressed him to explore and describe the other areas of the MPH model and as a result she was able to build a detailed and robust picture of John's situation. In particular she focused on developing a Projected, Micro, Hand picture, helping him to consider in detail just what the role of a personal coach would be and how this might impact on both his dream and the development work he would need to undertake.

7

Clarify – what is (really) going on?

The story so far

At this stage of the coaching partnership commitment has been established and both sides are confident of the chances of value being delivered. Building on this the coach now understands in some depth how the client feels, thinks and behaves, both in daily life and in relation to their coaching topic. The coach then developed a clear picture of the issues to be addressed and a compelling perfect picture that defines what the client wished to achieve.

Enter the Clarify stage

In the clarification stage we aim to delve further into the picture that the client has painted, to understand some of the deeper truths (both known and unknown) that might be preventing the client from resolving their issue. This is because coaching is often less about helping the client to do more of something or to do it better and more a simple case of asking the question, 'So what is stopping you?'

As the coach delves into the areas where limiting beliefs restrict performance, there is a chance that the client will seek to keep certain issues under wraps. Because the issues can be personal and in some cases embarrassing the coach needs to understand what issues the client is keeping from them and find a way to surface the issue for discussion.

The Fantasy Ladder

Argue for your limitations and sure enough, they're yours.

Richard Bach

We all have beliefs about ourselves and the world, but often these viewpoints can be inaccurate. For example, I spent 15 years working for a large company believing that I didn't have the confidence or competence to be able to branch out on my own. The trouble is that because I believed it as an absolute truth I shared this idea with others. They (in most cases) reinforced that belief by agreeing that I had become too entrenched in the business and could never survive. This fantasy became even further reinforced because I felt trapped and unhappy and so my performance dropped. Because of this my managers would give me a poor annual review and this in turn reinforced a belief that I was useless. No matter how many courses I went on, no matter how many qualifications I gained, and no matter how many good friends tried to counter this self-destruct button, I could not and would not erase the fantasy that I was unemployable and lucky to have a job.

Our life experiences often create a deep-seated boundary of what is and is not possible. While some of these ideas may be factual, many of them are often limiting beliefs. This might be the client who believes they can never be a good presenter; the one who doesn't believe that they can get promoted; or the housewife who says that she is and always will be 'just' a housewife. Conversely, it might be the team member who believes that they are better than the manager and should be doing their job (when in fact they are not), or the aspiring teenagers on TV who believe they are destined to be famous stars. Some of these erroneous fantasies are self-created, false beliefs that we have generated as the internal absolutes and autopilots create a false image. Other fantasies are blindly given to us as we associate with people who might also have deep self-limiting beliefs. Because they believe that 'life is hard' we unconsciously adopt their map of the world – scarily without even realizing it.

> **❝ Our life experiences often create a deep-seated boundary of what is and is not possible. ❞**

The trouble is that once the coach helps the client develop a clear picture of what they want the future to be like in the MPH stage, these limiting beliefs or fantasies kick in and cause the client to place blocks that prevent action. If we choose a goal of learning to ride a motorbike, which goes against our deep belief that we can't ride, our performance and progress are going to be affected. We may not consciously use the words 'can't ride', may never even think about it, but still, in our minds, we see ourselves in this category. Recognizing this is one of the most important steps on our way to delivering sustainable value – understanding that often the thing that holds us back most is just our own idea that we are not likely to succeed.

Once the coach helps the client to appreciate that the biggest block to their progression will be the negative fantasies they have created for themselves, they can begin to work on changing those preconceptions and so move forward. In this way, the client role at this stage is very much one of self-discovery.

Chris Argyris, a leading author in the field of human systems, identified how the shift from hard objective data to subjective fiction can quite rapidly take place over a number of stages:

- I see something happen that is quite factual.
- I select details from what I observe, based on my beliefs and values.
- I use these details and add my personal meanings, based on personal experiences.
- This view shifts from interpretation to hard fact.
- I take actions and change my behaviour, based on these new beliefs.

This can be characterized in the form of a ladder that people climb on their journey from clear objectivity to clouded subjectivity, as seen in Figure 7.1. At the bottom of the ladder is a fact or event that happens. The client then selects elements of the event and turns it into Faction, something that is basically true but is influenced and modified by our map of the world. The Faction turns into Fiction, as the biased story is translated into a distorted view of what happened – although some element of the fact can be found, you would have to dig quite deep to uncover the real events. Finally, the Fiction turns into Fantasy as the story takes on mythical status. This may be triggered by the original fact, but has nothing to do with it in terms of either content or detail.

The climb up the Fantasy Ladder doesn't have to involve other people. This is something that you do individually and often in a few seconds. Think about the last time you made a presentation. All is going well until you realize that the man at the end of the third row is not paying attention. You then realize that he is actually typing on his laptop. Immediately, the insecurity driver kicks in and you think that your presentation is failing. You

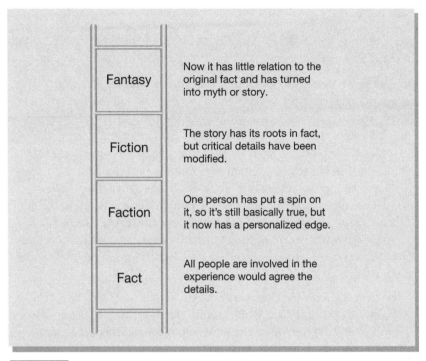

Figure 7.1   Fantasy Ladder

start to climb up to the Faction level as you conclude that other people are probably not interested either and are just looking interested to be polite. Then you reach the Fiction stage where you believe that your presentational style is all wrong. You're not clever enough, you look a mess and don't have any funny stories to draw upon like the really good presenters. By the end, you've made a headlong jump into Fantasy and decided that you'll never do any more of this type of presentation – you're not up to it and it's far better coming from someone who really knows what they are doing.

This leap up the ladder is a common event and one that people beat themselves up over on a daily basis. If not during a presentation then it might be how you react in a team meeting, at a family gathering, or at college. The point is that we often climb the ladder without any real need to. We let an insecurity and limited view of the world build conclusions that are unclear or totally false. In the above case, it might have been that the man at the end of the row was really enthused about the presentation and wanted to capture all the elements that weren't in the overheads. Unless you take time to climb down the ladder and operate at fact level, you'll be forever operating in fantasy land.

Climbing the ladder

The climb up the ladder is typically based upon three imperceptible and intrinsic processes:

- **Fact to Faction – Attenuation:** This occurs when we selectively pay attention to certain aspects of our experience and not others. There is evidence that the central nervous system is being fed more than two million bits of information every second. If we ever tried to understand, process and consciously manage this information as it arrived into our sensory system we would be overwhelmed and never be able to function at an efficient level. This is where the process of attenuation occurs. Our personal operating system acts as a screening mechanism enabling us to function at peak efficiency. Without attenuation where certain pieces of sensory data are turned down, our conscious mind would be faced with too much information to handle all at once.

- **Faction to Fiction – Alteration:** Have you ever wondered how two people watching the same film can see the same story but come away with totally different ideas about what happened? This occurs when we take in sensory data but ascribe different values to it based upon our map of the world. When I'm on my bike and I see a group of Harley Davidson riders coming down the street I will wave and see whether I recognize anyone. However, the driver who has just read Sonny Barger's[1] book on Hell's Angels might instantly think of them as riders out to wreak damage in the neighbourhood.

- **Fiction to Fantasy – Amplification:** This is where we draw global conclusions based on one or two experiences and ascribe an absolute truth to them. This is the fun point when the new comedian gets a great round of applause on their first time out. The downside of this is that when erroneous negative thoughts are passed through the amplification filter they become global generalizations – facts that are always true! The danger is that the aspiring comedian builds and believes a sense of greatness that is not quite true, especially since all the people in the audience at the first gig were his friends and family.

> **We attenuate, alter and amplify the incoming sensory data.**

1 Barger, Sonny (2001) *Hell's Angel: The Life and Times of Sonny Barger and the Hell's Angels Motorcycle Club*, Fourth Estate.

This process of filtering determines how we see the world, how we make choices and hence how we behave. In order to process any experience or event, we attenuate, alter and amplify the incoming sensory data. This modification can happen in the space of seconds or it can take months or years to create a fantasy about ourselves. The route can be seen in Figure 7.2.

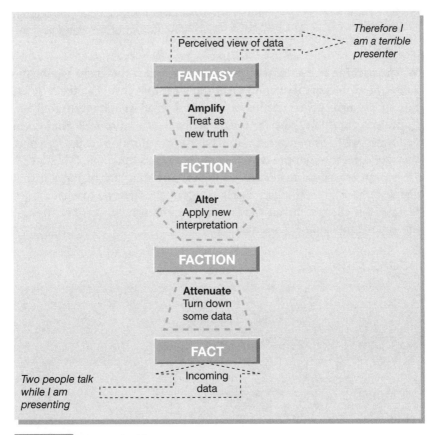

Figure 7.2 Fantasy Ladder

The Fantasy Ladder can be seen to occur for all people in everyday situations:

■ New manager doing a presentation to the board and two directors begin talking – Fantasy: I am not a good presenter and will never do this again.

■ Teenager walks across the dance floor and is rejected by a girl in front of friends – Fantasy: I am ugly, spotty and no one will ever want to go out with me.

- Someone recently made redundant fails interview for a job – Fantasy: I am and always will be unemployable.

- Recent divorcee goes speed dating and doesn't get to meet anyone – Fantasy: this is it, divorced with three kids to look after alone for the rest of my life.

- New employee gets a roasting by the manager for making a mistake with the paperwork – Fantasy: I have really messed up and they will let me go at the end of the week.

When coaching it is important to understand how the client climbs the ladder, how quickly they get up there and what they do once they're at the top. For example, give them one word and ask them what it means to them. Consider a word like 'job'. Do they describe it as a set of tasks that when performed well form one of the assets of the organization? Is it something they do to get through the day? Is it a life or death situation? Is it slavery? Or is it an escape from the kids at home? The spin and perception that people place on something as simple as this might offer the coach a chance to map the client's change ladder and, importantly, understand how it impacts the topic under consideration.

Embedded fantasies

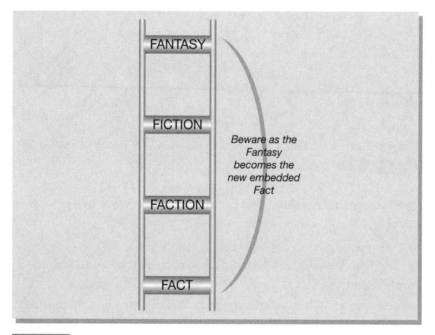

Figure 7.3   Embedded fantasies

This far in the outline of the Fantasy Ladder we have been looking at the processes that get people to the top. The real difficulty arises when people create a fantasy or belief about themselves and it begins to stick (Figure 7.3). So the teenager who is rejected by someone at the dance may really begin to believe that his fantasies are facts. As a consequence he doesn't go out, avoids people and ends up as a recluse. Or the person made redundant decides to give up looking for meaningful work and just takes a get-by job because they feel that their skills and knowledge are not in demand in the current marketplace. As a coach you will have to identify these embedded fantasies and find ways to address them.

As we begin to explore the type of embedded fantasies it becomes possible to identify four common patterns that people can develop, as seen in Figure 7.4. These embedded beliefs can sometimes be really clear and obvious when you first meet the client, often from the language being used. Other times they are quite subtle and the coach will need to delve deeply to uncover and surface the shadows.

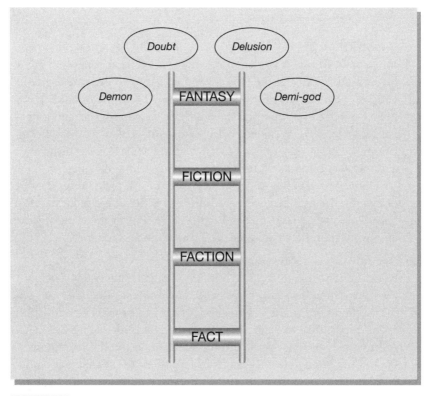

Figure 7.4   Common fantasies

The four fantasy domains can be described as follows:

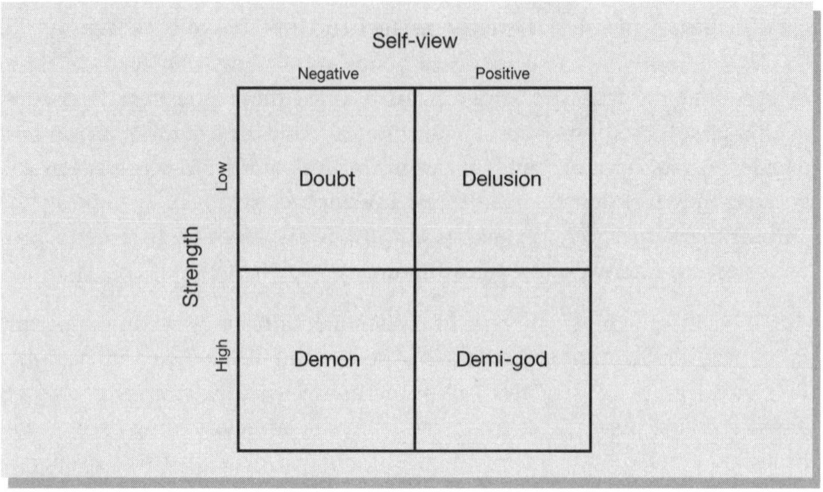

Figure 7.5   The four fantasy domains

- **Doubt:** This is the 16-year-old girl who loves singing and wants to get into a band who sees a video of herself in a karaoke competition on holiday. On looking at the tape she self-judges to an extreme degree and forms a distorted view of her capability. As such, self-doubt creeps in and she begins to question her ability to take up singing and join a band. However, what she has failed to take into account is that it was two in the morning and the DJ was shouting while she was using an audio system that harked back to the dark ages in terms of technical standards. She 'chooses' to ignore this and instead picks up on the one or two vocal slips. The good news with this is that the coach can fairly readily resolve the issue by helping the client look again at the video and really appreciate the potential in the vocal performance.

- **Demon:** This is the 16-year-old girl who becomes a 32-year-old woman, married with children and full of regrets that she was never good enough to be a singer in a band. The trouble is that after 16 years of self-conditioning the coach will have a tough time trying to help the client resolve this problem. In an ideal world it is resolvable, but in reality it may be that the client runs out of hope and the coach runs out of time to help shift this demon. This is not to say that it shouldn't be addressed – quite the contrary – just beware of the time and energy it may take to resolve.

▨ **Delusion:** This is the opposite of the Doubt model. In this case this is the 16-year-old who is learning to play bass and joins a school band. He really believes they are great as the band gets lots of gigs and everyone tells the bass player how good he is. What he doesn't take into account is that the other guitarists in the band are all too happy to praise him because they don't want to get pushed on to the bass guitar (often deemed to be the less sexy instrument). So he lives in this world where he is the new rock star. This is fine where it is a fun dream or fantasy; the problem arises when he believes all the self-talk and decides to cancel his college studies as surely he will be good enough to become a professional musician. Now this is not to suggest that the coach's job is to damp anyone's dream – but they are there to ensure that such choices are made on the basis of fact and not fantasy. If the coach is working with this type of client, they need to ensure that tangible and objective data is fed back to the client so that the client can make an informed choice and not one based on fantasies that have been fuelled by others' willingness to lie and their own willingness to make false assumptions about themselves.

▨ **Demi-god:** Think of a famous sports star, rock icon or politician and who they surround themselves with. Often it is people who will happily reinforce the personal belief system about how great they are and of course how they will continue to be a huge star for the next 20 years. Imagine that this young bass player has very rich parents. They can't tell one bass guitarist from the next and so believe his fantasies. In doing this they buy him a full bass rig and PA system. The net result is that all the local bands are crying out for his services – not because of his skills but because of what he brings to the party. The result is that after many years of being associated with lackeys and false supporters his delusional view is reinforced and he becomes a Demi-god, with absolute belief in his ability. This is a really hard one for the coach to deal with and can often be found at work with people who are frustrated when they don't get promoted and have a cast-iron belief in the fact that they are actually better than their boss. The coach may well have to get them to look face on in the mirror and really accept their faults. This is no mean feat and in many cases the coach will meet a client who absolutely refuses to look in the mirror or who sees a princess even when presented with a picture of an ugly witch.

The issue surrounding all four fantasy segments is how the coach can help move the client from a position of Fiction, Faction or Fantasy and get them to on a Fact-based view of the world. Although the next section begins to consider one of the underlying factors that can help with this, there is one core principle that underlies all attempts to move the client from Fantasy to Fact: you can't!

You, the coach, can never move anyone!

The coach has no ability or right to pull the client down the Fantasy Ladder. If the coach seeks to make the choice for the client then they are implicitly embedding a sense of dependence from the outset of the relationship. You might be able to drag them down, but like a rubber band there is every chance that they will rebound up there again once the coach is not around. Just imagine someone who has a fear of heights stuck at the top of a ladder. If a fireman climbs up to help the person down and tries to tug at them, in most cases the person will grip even tighter as fear kicks in. The clever fireman will instead coach the person and help them climb down themselves with confidence, but the fireman is there just in case they start to fall.

> **The coach has no ability or right to pull the client down the Fantasy Ladder.**

Hence the coach's role in helping someone climb down the Fantasy Ladder is to accept that they can never make the person come down and that their role is to help the client find their own way down the steps. They will do this through the careful use of feedback and questioning and, importantly, provide a safe environment in which this can happen. The structure of the questioning process is considered in the next section.

From Fantasy to Fact

Just to recap, we said that three specific processes can occur that help move the client up the ladder, namely:

- Attenuation – turn down some incoming data and focus on just a small area of information.

- Alteration – reinterpreting what the data means based on personal experience.

- Amplification – generalizing and making this reframed viewpoint a fundamental truth.

As the coach tries to help the client climb down the Fantasy Ladder, a key component of the questioning strategy will be to reverse these three processes, to seek to minimize and where possible counteract the effect that the cognitive process has had in distorting the client's view of themselves and others.

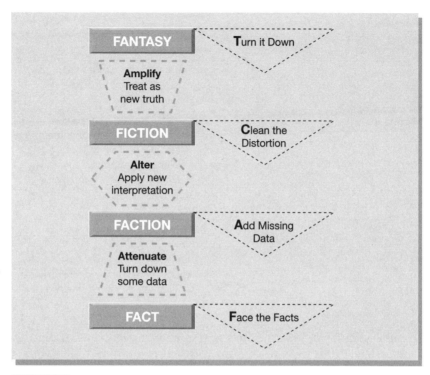

Figure 7.6   Climbing down the Fantasy Ladder

The three key questioning activities used to counteract the processes can be seen in Figure 7.6. This is the 'FACT' model and follows the pattern shown in Table 7.1.

Table 7.1   The FACT model

Ladder force	Counter force	Question description
Amplification	Turn it down	Try to strip away the globalization and generalization by questioning whether this 'always happens', 'will it always be true?' and 'can it never be wrong?'.
Alteration	Clean the distortion	Seek to understand where the distortion has occurred and determine why the client has formed a specific opinion about the observed data. Question what makes this version of events true over and above another interpretation. Ask, 'What makes you think that?' and 'Why is that so?' The coach might suggest alternative

Table 7.1	Contiinued	
Ladder force	*Counter force*	*Question description*
		interpretations of the same data at this point to help the client broaden their viewpoint.
Attenuation	Add missing data	Look at the source of the data to understand what they have tuned out. Seek to include other data from that same event and help them to take a wider and more objective view of the situation. Ask, 'How might others view this?' or 'What else happened?'
	Face the facts	At this point they should be down the ladder with a full appreciation of what happened. The coach's role now is to help the client face the facts and see to what extent their perception of a situation is correct or incorrect.

It is the final step of 'Face the Facts' that is quite important and potentially quite difficult. It is here that the client who believed they were terrible at presenting might find that in fact they are OK, but they might also find that they are really bad. This is where the client has to look in the mirror and deal with and confront so many of the home truths they may have buried for years. So the client who struggled to lose weight (and has blamed their busy work schedule) may have to finally accept that they are addicted to food and can no longer live a lie, blaming others for their compulsive behaviour.

I would also highlight that the coach must include themselves in the requirement to climb down the Fantasy Ladder. Unless they are a robot, all coaches will form automatic judgements and inferences about the client and the picture they tell. The moment the client walks through the door the coach will build a mental assumption about the person that is based on their speech patterns, accent, clothes, car that is parked outside and a host of seemingly small factors that help make up who we are. The coach must learn to curb these assumptions and not build unconscious fantasies about the client that will impact the service they provide.

Hence, this stage of the coaching cycle might well prove diffcult for many clients and coaches because it demands that both have the time and courage to be really open and reflective about themselves and each other. They must develop the ability to recognize and free themselves from any limiting beliefs, assumptions and logical comfort zones. As well as time and courage, this will demand humility from both players to re-examine embedded inferences, along with the capability to make any needed shifts in how they view the world. However, the coach's ability to share how they map, monitor and manage their fantasies can offer a terrific opportunity to model good behaviour with the client and ideally strip away any fear they may have in reflecting on what they thought were facts.

Coaching questions

Turn it down
- Does this always happen? How do you know?
- Are you sure this is always the case?
- Are there times when this isn't true?
- Can you give one example of when it worked well?
- Could you clarify what you mean when you say that?

Clean the distortion
- Can you run me through your viewpoint and why you believe certain things?
- How did we get from those facts to the current situation?
- What leads you to believe this?
- Can you help me understand your thinking here?
- I'd like to understand more. What leads you to believe . . .?
- Where does your reasoning go next?
- What if this were not true?

Add missing data
- What actually happened?
- How would others describe it?
- What else has been considered?
- Is there any way we could get to similar perspectives?

Face the facts
- What do you think are the facts of the situation?
- Do you believe that view is correct?
- Will you believe it the next time the problem occurs or will you go back to the old way of thinking?

Surface the shadows

The secret of staying young is to live honestly, eat slowly, and lie about your age.

Lucille Ball

As the coach seeks to help the client delve into the deeper areas and understand what blockages are preventing them from making the change, there is every likelihood that the client will resist any action to surface such sensitive areas. It is these shadow factors that are often the most important and need surfacing as soon as possible in the relationship.

A definition of shadow factors in a coaching partnership might be all the important information that does not get identified, discussed and managed in the open. The shadow side deals with the covert, the undiscussed, the undiscussable and the unmentionable.[2] These sit in the shade of the person and appear only when a light is deliberately shone upon them. An example of the shadow areas can be seen in Figure 7.7.

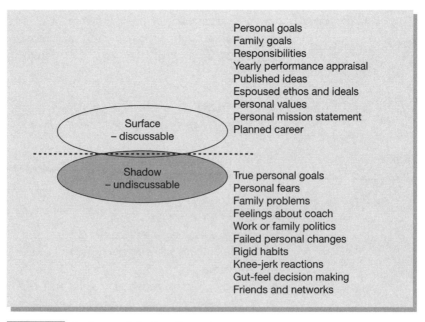

Personal goals
Family goals
Responsibilities
Yearly performance appraisal
Published ideas
Espoused ethos and ideals
Personal values
Personal mission statement
Planned career

Surface
– discussable

Shadow
– undiscussable

True personal goals
Personal fears
Family problems
Feelings about coach
Work or family politics
Failed personal changes
Rigid habits
Knee-jerk reactions
Gut-feel decision making
Friends and networks

Figure 7.7   Surface and shadow dimensions

2 Egan, Gerard (1994) *Working the Shadow Side*, Jossey Bass, 1994, page 35.

Shadows exist in coaching relationships because people have an instinctive desire to protect themselves from emotional pain or embarrassment. This is because most people choose to talk about things that will allow them to look favourable rather than surfacing issues that might lead to confrontation and upheaval.

> **Often, our immune system becomes highly effective in resisting bad news.**

However, although the coach may be aware of shadows within their client relationship, moving them to the surface can be somewhat difficult. Often, our immune system becomes highly effective in resisting bad news and in many cases we chastise or shun any individual who tries to bring it to the surface. Their act of making the 'undiscussable discussable' can be seen as painful, difficult and in many cases downright threatening.

Although the coach might think they are close enough to the client to be able to explore areas that are potentially sensitive, they are unlikely to be so emotionally connected with them that they are prepared to share all of their personal shadows. For example, think about the people in your life whom you trust and are close to. Do you really share everything with them? Even all the secret fear, dreams and fantasies? There are some things that are so deep we might never tell anyone but our closest soul mate. But what if this issue is significant and has a major impact on the topic being coached?

Argyris (1992)[3] suggests that there is a fundamental set of behavioural rules that drive shadow behaviour and they cross all nations and cultures. People keep these rules in their heads to help deal with embarrassment or threat:

- Bypass embarrassment or threat whenever possible.
- Act as if you are not bypassing them.
- Do not discuss this bypassing while it is happening.
- Do not discuss the undiscussability of the undiscussable.

In tacitly following these four rules, people will inherently lock themselves into a 'I know it's true because I say so' style of behaviour. The problem surfaces when you attempt to tackle any of these four rules head-on – asking people to clarify what the problem is and trying to discuss some of the deeper issues as part of the diagnostic process. All of these are likely to trigger some form of defensive reaction that in turn drives up the shadows.

---

3 Argyris, C. and Schon, D.A. (1992) *Theory in Practice: Increasing Professional Effectiveness*, Jossey Bass Wiley.

The danger is that as the coach seeks to surface the shadows, unless they are well practised in this skilful art it can seem fumbling and clumsy. It's just like the first teenage date where both are second-guessing each other – do they get close enough to touch? Who holds hands first? When saying goodbye is it a single peck on the cheek or a full-on kiss? In the same way, the early meetings with a client can end up as a series of fumbling encounters, where both people try to understand the needs and goals of the other. Part of the reason why this dilemma occurs is because we try to satisfy needs on two levels – the surface and the shadow. The surface issues are considered on an open and level playing field and the shadow issues are the factors that both sides choose to hide from each other.

In a typical coaching engagement, you might offer what appears to be a practical and sensible set of questions but the client rebuffs with procrastination and delaying arguments. Are these rebuttals coming from the reasoned head of the client or are shadow concerns forcing unrelated and possibly irrelevant issues to the surface?

Crucially, when developing a relationship with the client, you must listen to what they say and, more importantly, watch what they do. The pained facial expression as your client talks about the people they work with or the involuntary eye movement as the topic is discussed are valuable indicators that highlight a possible shadow issue. These types of subtle indicators will not automatically tell you about the deeper issues at play, but they might offer signals that the topic could be explored further to pull out any shadow factors.

This is why the clarification stage is often very difficult but when successful can unearth all the issues that have caused a blockage in the first place. It is difficult because the client will naturally enough seek to defend their deep-seated thoughts and feelings, but once the coach is able to get close enough to help bring them to the surface it is common for the client to suddenly recognize that they don't need coaching because all of the blockages are internal and they have disappeared once surfaced. Very often just helping the client to recognize that they are scared of taking a certain action rather than finding excuses why they can't do it is sufficient for them to choose to move forward. As with an alcoholic or drug addict, often the first and hardest step is for them to admit that they are addicted. Once they have voiced this, the solution can develop with greater speed and clarity.

Shadow steps

However, in seeking to surface the shadows it is important to understand that they are not always black and white issues. The greyness can often be less in the nature of the topic but rather in the people the client is prepared to share the topic with. There are some things that are so deep that the client doesn't even know that they will not share them with others. These are the suppressed issues. Yet there are others things that people will happily share with anyone, as the increase in TV discussion shows seems to indicate – where people are happy to bare their emotions, thoughts and, in many cases, bodily parts.

But let's start with the deepest shadow level: for example, anger might be considered as a topic that is often suppressed. Many people believe that nearly every addict has anger issues, some buried so deeply that the client is not only unaware of them but may have developed sophisticated defence mechanisms that make it difficult to surface them. Consider the client who perceives that she is being treated unfairly; she might naturally display anger towards her manager. If the manager acknowledges the person's anger and allows it to be expressed in a one-to-one meeting, the energy dissipates and they are able to move on. If, however, the manager does not see the deep anger or is not prepared to allow it to surface, energy must then be dispersed internally, for it has to go somewhere. As a result she may internalize all her anger, or displace it on to a less formidable target such as her partner or children. Alternatively she might suppress the anger through the use of drugs and alcohol. Sooner or later, this solution will always end in problems. Either the de-inhibiting effects of the chemicals will allow the suppressed feelings to release in an uncontrolled manner or the anger will bury deeper and lead to stress-related symptoms.

> **Many people believe that nearly every addict has anger issues.**

This can be compared to the child who rather than cleaning the bedroom properly takes the easy route and just stuffs all the dirty washing, left-over chicken portions and discarded pizzas under the bed. Eventually it will become hard to walk into the room without smelling the mess and noticing the mice and rats chasing across the floor. Unless some serious cleaning effort is undertaken, it will soon become a challenge even to consider clearing under the bed for fear of being bitten.

The next level up the shadow steps might be those things we keep secret, i.e. we know them but choose to tell no one. This might be the sexual thoughts about a neighbour, the minor indiscretion from last year's Christmas party or a dream of becoming the next person to climb a mountain or bungee-jump off the Eiffel Tower.

We then move up the steps to the safe level, which are those things that we choose to share with a trusted group – a select band of people who would never ever share the topic further. This group might be just one person, but it is important because of the defined boundary based on trust. The next step up again takes us to the select level, which is similar to the safe step but is released to a community of people which is larger in size, and hence the trust funds and distribution rights are more blurred. At this level the person is saying, I don't want to broadcast this to the world but I am happy for you to disclose it to anyone you know. So the surfacing of this shadow topic is based on the premise of trusting the colleagues of the people you have trusted. Finally, we have the surface level, where the client has no reservation about sharing this particular topic: it is an open agenda that is unlimited and unbounded.

The shadow steps seen in Figure 7.8 can show how the coach's goal is to help the client increase their level of exposure – but crucially only on those topics that are pertinent to the chosen coaching subject. This is not an exercise in mass disclosure where the coach fervently seeks to unearth all the client's deep psychological factors. This might be viewed more as therapy and this is not the objective within this book. This is a coaching framework and the coach must be very careful of how far they seek to surface the shadows.

The key words are always respect, relevance and responsibility. The coach must respect the client's position and always accept that the client surfaces what they want to surface. Once released it is treated with reverence and dignity. Second, the coach must always ask the question, 'How does surfacing information around this topic help move the client towards their goal?' If it doesn't, leave it alone. Finally, the coach is in a position of immense power; by virtue of their position they can unknowingly push the client way beyond a position where they originally intended to go. It is for this reason that the coach must be cognisant of their responsibility to never let the client move into a position of exposure that would be emotionally harmful. An acid test for this is to always question whether the client will later regret surfacing this shadow. If the answer is 'yes' then my belief is that the coach has an ethical responsibility not to progress along that route. However, they might explain to the client that they are consciously not seeking to surface a particular topic area because the client may later regret it. This allows the client to reflect on the issue and come to their own conclusion as to whether it has relevance to their particular topic.

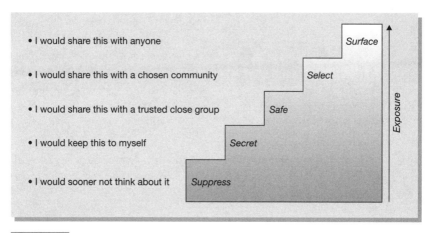

Figure 7.8   Shadow steps

Shadow maps

When looking at the notion of shadows, let's be clear that it is not just the client with shadows. The coach will have levels of undiscussable topics that link to the shadow steps. These might be a deep fear of failure (Suppressed); the fact that they sometimes get really fed up with clients who seem to whinge (Secret); the different categories they put clients in (Safe); the marketing process they use (Select); and their coaching process (Surface). In recognizing that the coach and client both have shadows to resolve, it is important to map and understand how they interrelate and importantly if there are areas where conflict might arise.

The shadow map is a simple tool that allows you to understand what shadows might reside between the coach and the client. Once the shadows are mapped it can be easier for the coach to take remedial action to surface the factors that need to be addressed.

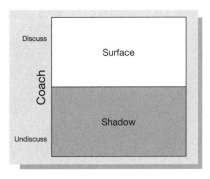

In the first case the coach must be able to reflect on what shadow issue they have in relation to the client and the project. At a surface level you might be prepared to talk about the engagement plan, fees, your skills set and other clients with whom you have worked on similar projects. However, shadows for the coach might be the fact that you have taken the client on because of pressure from a colleague or maybe you have contracted to support another colleague at the same time and so will need to split your time across two key clients who will be sharing information about each other.

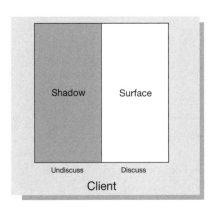

The client's surface issues may be their personal goals and their career story. The shadow issues might be the fact that they know that they will be leaving the company in six months, or that they don't really think much of the coach.

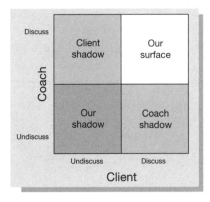

Once the coach and client come together, we end up with a combination of four constructs: the things neither wants to discuss, the things the client will discuss and the coach will not, the things the coach will discuss and the client will not, and the things that both will happily discuss. The resulting four segments are not fixed elements, rather they change in size depending upon the level of disclosure and willingness to share undiscussables by the client and coach. As both players flex their degree of discussables, so the shape of the shadow map will vary.

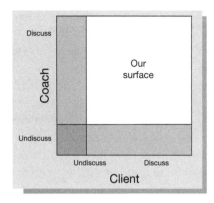

When the shadow map has this shape the suggestion is that both client and coach are open in their interaction. The surface area offers plenty of space for both to share the discussable items and so effect a robust clarification stage. The one risk with this shape is of being lulled into a false sense of security – like the married couple who are proud of their relationship and proclaim their openness to the world, only to find out that one of them has a deep secret that when surfaced blows the whole relationship apart. Although the bottom left box is only small, it can contain dangerous viral spores that can kill a relationship.

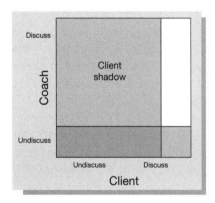

This shape indicates a client who has deep undiscussable issues. An example of this might be the client who is being coached by their line manager. The manager is diligently working with them to help address a number of performance issues that have surfaced in recent months. The coach has built a robust and detailed picture of the team member's situation, understands their 3D drivers and has agreed a clear perfect picture. The trouble is that the client has another job lined up – but can't tell the manager because it doesn't start for another four months.

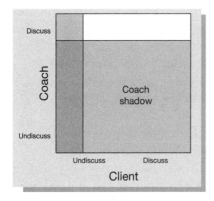

With this shape, the client is happy to disclose and share many things but the coach is closing down and is not happy to share what they are thinking and feeling. This first question is, why? What is causing them to be holding back and creating undiscussables in the relationship? Second, what does this large shadow box contain and are there elements in there that can be destructive for the engagement?

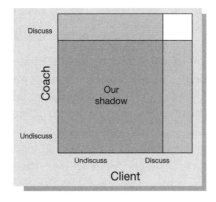

This is the killer shape, where both the client and coach are limiting their level of disclosure. Now, if this is the start of the relationship, it is a shape that might be expected and possibly makes sense as both sides might have sensitivities to protect. However, if this shape exists part way through the engagement, this is a dangerous sign as neither party is prepared to open up and share their thoughts and feelings. An example of this shape can be found when a line manager is trying to coach a member of the team or a parent seeks to coach one of their teenage children, because both players have so many other issues going on outside of the coaching topic.

The suggestion is that effective coaching clarification can only really take place when the (relevant) shadow has been surfaced and the coach and client are free to really understand what is going on. The art of shadow mapping comes in the ability to move two key lines within the shadow map, shown in Figure 7.9.

Although there will always be a variety of strategies that can be used to open up the surface area and shrink the shadow area, they will be primarily dependent upon the ability to move the two lines in the direction shown by the arrows. The coach must be able to move their line from top to bottom to make more things discussable and the client must be helped to move the line from right to left and do the same.

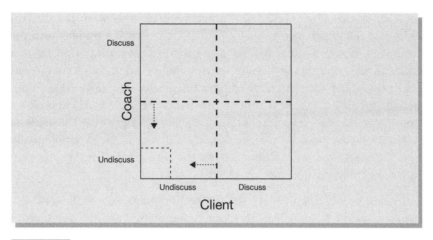

Figure 7.9   Moving the shadow map

Sabotage secrets

Finally, beware the sabotage factors that have the potential to destroy a coaching relationship. The sabotage secrets are those shadow factors that sit deep in the bottom left-hand corner of the shadow map (Figure 7.10).

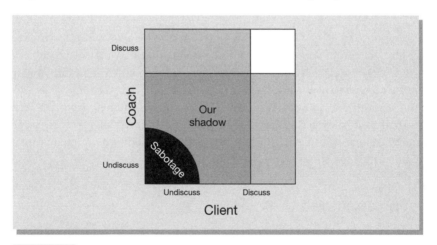

Figure 7.10   Coach–client shadow map

The problem is they are buried so deep that neither the client nor the coach really wants them to be surfaced. This might be seen where the coach is a manager in a large organization and they are coaching someone as part of a career development plan. The overt goal is terrific because the client is part of a senior manager development programme and the coach is a director who has the experience to really help the client make inroads into the company. However, what neither is prepared to mention is the fact that company revenues have fallen for the past three years, the customer base is contracting and there is an air of consolidation in the market. They both fear that their joint careers in the company may be short-lived but both are too scared to surface it for fear of the emotions it might release. The problem is that if neither has the courage to surface this issue they are potentially wasting their time by coaching around the wrong topic and maybe even damaging their relationship.

Although people often believe that by keeping these potentially awkward issues at a deep shadow level they can be forgotten, I am not convinced. I believe that when this happens there will be leakage. This leakage might be nervousness when around certain people, potential panic when dealing with certain infor-

> **ff The process of bringing them to the surface can also be destructive. JJ**

mation, and the constant fear of disclosure that leads to sleepless nights. The paradox is that although they can be destructive when hidden, the process of bringing them to the surface can also be destructive. There is no right answer; the trick is just to be aware that they can exist for many people and organizations and be prepared to deal with them.

Please note that very few coaches are trained to be able to deal with deep cognitive, emotional or behavioural problems that may surface when they try to clarify a client's needs. It is vital that, if faced with a situation you are not equipped to deal with, you act responsibly and advise the client to seek the appropriate, professional help. Unless you are trained, however well intentioned your actions, you may do more harm than good. In some circumstances it can pay to agree this with the client when drawing up a contract for the coaching engagement.

Surfacing strategies

Often knowing that the shadows are there can be the easy part, the difficult element comes in trying to help and encourage the client to surface them. For example, take any 16-year-old boy or girl and you can reasonably predict the shadows they have with their parents, pick any one of drink, drugs, disease and debt. This is not to suggest that all parent/child relationships are like this, but there is a range of common issues that many parents will find a challenge to talk about with their children. Alternatively, when running a training programme I can assume that a range of common shadows will exist in the room, for example, people who have been 'sent' and don't want to be there, those who need to leave early but don't like to mention it, those with a hangover. In a team event it can be the underlying relationship niggles that no one is talking about or the fact that everyone is playing the 'pacify the boss' game. Hence spotting the shadows can be easy – but just how do we surface them?

The coach needs to develop a set of shadow strategies. These are disclosure processes that will allow them to unearth and expose areas of potential liability. Although the emotional act of making the undiscussable discussable can be difficult, there are some simple tools that you can employ to help this process (Figure 7.11).

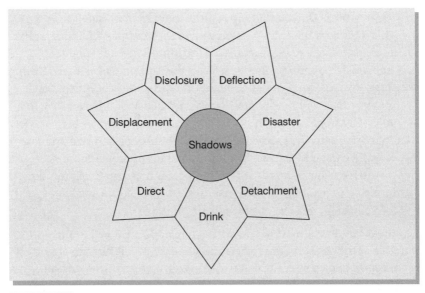

Figure 7.11   Surfacing strategies

■ **Disclosure:** This is possibly one of the most powerful and effective ways to open up the shadow area. If you are with someone who really doesn't want to open up (and we all generally know this when it is happening to us), be brave and open up to him or her. Find things that maybe you weren't going to share with them and explain that it is quite a deep feeling but that you want to share it with them so as to help the relationship develop. The upside is that by sharing this and demonstrating that you trust them they might reciprocate and begin to open up. The downside is that they may simply soak up all your shadows and give nothing back. Only you can decide how far to go with this, but if you feel that nothing is being reciprocated then in many cases it might be prudent to pull back for a while and try an alternative strategy.

▣ **Deflection:** This is a displacement process often used in marketing. Imagine you are walking down the street and a researcher enquires whether they can ask some questions. They want to test out a new perfume or aftershave and understand whether people believe it will make them smell sexier. Now if someone sprays this on you and says, 'Do you feel sexier?' – the chances are that it can be really awkward to answer truthfully because you feel embarrassed. However, if the researcher lets you smell the perfume and then shows you a picture of someone wearing the scent or aftershave, you are more likely to answer the question, 'Do you think that this will make them smell sexier?' This is because the focus of attention has been displaced. It has created a safe haven where you can answer truthfully without being embarrassed. In the same way, if you are with someone who is showing signs of shadows, then talk about another friend of yours who has a problem they will not share with anyone. Talk about this and say that you really want to help this person but are not sure of the best way to do it. Alternatively, maybe talk about a TV show or film that you saw recently where the characters caused all kinds of problems for themselves simply because they didn't open up when it was important. By virtue of making the shadows discussable it may create a safe house for your friend to start to surface some of their issues.

▣ **Disaster:** Sometimes there is nothing as 'good' as a 'bad' thing. Just look at the disaster films, where the standard plot is meet in airport reception; have safe, comfortable chats; take off in plane; disaster comes along; people express real feelings; all saved – then they walk away better people. The challenge for the coach is to maybe tap into the disaster model – to create a situation where people feel some of the pain associated with holding back and then use this as a platform to surface the shadows. Again this can be risky and should be treated with some trepidation because everything might come out in a rush and then you end up with buckets of shadows that you don't know how to deal with. But it can be a valuable way in which to surface some deep issues that can't seem to get unblocked.

▣ **Displacement:** All human beings will vent inner rage and frustration towards others. If late for a meeting because of a traffic jam I might blow up. I might express anger to my colleagues on the injustice of the situation and get angry about anything now. One way of surfacing the shadows can be to help this to happen – help the client surface undiscussables by venting their rage at another (hopefully inanimate) thing. It is as if the client's emotional shadows can be held in a storage tank for a period of time and then released when safe.

■ **Detachment:** We can see ourselves from a number of perspectives. There is the first-person position when we talk from a subjective perspective, then there is the second-person position where we move into a more objective role. In doing this we encourage the client to stop using the 'I' word and to step outside of themselves and imagine that they are a detached observer. They are then encouraged to use the 'They' type description – describing how the person feels and the thoughts they might be having.

■ **Direct:** If your relationship is strong enough then sometimes you just have to tell it as you see it. Maybe there isn't time to pussyfoot around and you just have to go for it. Sometimes when I'm running a course where I feel there are underlying issues in the room, it is easier to just say what I feel. Although the group may reject the approach and say there are no problems, at least the item is on the agenda for discussion and I can pick up on it over coffee or in the corridor discussions.

■ **Drink:** This might be drink in the form of alcohol used to liberate the mouth muscle and open up suppressed areas. Alternatively it might be a nice grande latte coffee. Simply taking someone out of the work environment and dropping into a coffee shop can change the ambiance surrounding the coaching session and create an environment where people will open up.

As with all surfacing strategies, the objective is to create an emotional connection that will in turn allow you to clarify what is really going on. The danger with these types of strategies is they can be viewed and used as manipulative tools. This is a dangerous game to play and one that is diametrically opposite to the core principles of the Collaborative Coaching framework. My advice is to use the strategies if they help to build effective relationships. But always be open about the use of the strategy and never try to use it in a covert or duplicitous way.

Finally, beware of the shadows as they can and often do impact the nature of your relationship with the client. There is and always should be a clear and pronounced line that is never crossed, i.e. the professional–personal line. The coach is there to be a helper and not a friend and blurring of this boundary will generally cause a problem. The danger is that once you have entered the shadow arena in which the client regards you as their friend, all of their life's problems might start to surface. In doing this you might take that difficult step from a professional relationship to a personal one. Once in this area it can be difficult to move back into the professional one. The consequence is that you gain a new friend but lose a client. Always seek to keep clear separation of the two roles and ensure that the client understands the ethical and practical need for the separation to exist.

But the good news is . . .

Although the last statement can make the shadow area seem terribly daunting and foreboding, the good news is that where the coach and client are willing and able to surface some of these undiscussables, a huge weight is taken off both the relationship and the issue being considered. Think about the child who has smashed a window and is too frightened to tell his parents, the manager anxiously waiting to meet for her annual review, or the workshow presenter who gingerly picks up the course reviews left by the delegates. All of these areas have potential shadows that can create tremendous anxiety. But in most cases it is a case of better out than in. We see this with most cases of addiction where the first and most crucial step is getting to a point where the person can admit they have a problem. At this point they can put aside the childish games and excuses that have driven their life since the start of the addiction, and when this happens it is often possible to see a transformation in the person as a physical weight is lifted from their shoulders.

> **All of these areas have potential shadows that can create tremendous anxiety.**

The act of freeing the weight by surfacing these shadows can in many cases lead to a resolution of the issue without any great need for further support: when the client understands that the supposed problem with their manager is in fact a deep resentment they had buried because the manager used to work for them when they first started the company; or the marathon runner who has been struggling to hit the times she made in previous years suddenly accepts that age comes to everyone and that rather than trying to tease a few more months out of her frame it makes sense to accept that she is now in the veteran league; or the married couple who have been sniping at each other for years finally surface the fact that the affair one of them had many years ago is acting as a cancer in their relationship and that only by talking about it will they be able to move forward.

To really make inroads into the shadow areas all the coach and client need are two guiding beacons – courage and consideration. It is impossible to deny that in most cases entering the shadow areas needs a great deal of courage because it will in most cases surface huge amounts of emotion (both positive and negative) and carries with it a risk of unleashing issues and problems that neither coach nor client realized existed. But this must be done with amazing care and consideration. The coach must understand what pain the act might involve and be prepared to offer unlimited support for the client as they enter the sometimes alien world of honest self-reflection. However, when handled with care, the benefits far outweigh the risk of entering such areas.

Coaching questions

Shadow steps
- Are you happy to share your situation with everyone?
- Who are you not prepared to share it with? Why?
- What is the consequence of not sharing this with people?
- Are there any issues that you might not wish to share with me?

Shadow map
- Looking back, what issues caused previous personal changes to go wrong?
- What would others say is the thing that will inhibit the change you plan to make?
- Is there anything about our relationship that you think we might need to address?
- What is your greatest fear about this change?

John's journey

In listening to John paint his picture, two clear things stood out for Julie. The first was limiting beliefs in the way that he described what he could realistically do as a personal trainer and how much he could earn as a consequence. There was a high level of self-doubt that bordered on a demon that could stymie his move into the new market. Julie spent some time challenging John's view about his capability. She began to understand that much of the doubt had been embedded over many years of working in an organization that focused on the achievement of an agreed performance and did not really seek to unleash potential. At work John was used to setting safe boundaries and targets, ones that he knew

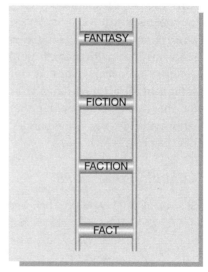

Fantasy Ladder

could be achieved since that is what had been the cultural norm in the company. In helping make John aware of these limiting beliefs she was able to help him open out his understanding of himself, his potential capability and what he might be able to achieve if he started to believe in himself.

The second issue that popped out from the Fantasy Ladder was a potentially dangerous delusion. John was convinced it would be easy to get new clients. John believed that all he needed to do was advertise in the paper and put a few cards in newsagents' windows and work would come rolling in. Julie challenged these presumptions quite heavily and asked John whether he felt that this was true for all personal trainers, how he knew that this was the best approach and where his evidence came from that this would be an easy process.

At the end of the session John was a lot clearer about the picture he had painted and had begun to include a level of pragmatic reality into the picture. The power of Julie's approach was that at no time did she tell him that he was wrong – she simply challenged his maps of the world and effectively asked him to explain how he knew what he knew and how he knew that it was a fact and not a self-driven fantasy.

Once Julie had helped John to build a richer and more detailed map of his situation, she then wanted to ensure that no time bombs existed that might explode later in the journey. She was conscious that John was planning to make a huge change in his life and one that came with a fair degree of potential risk.

Julie wanted to help John unearth and share some of his deeper fears or concerns about the venture so that they could understand how to either resolve them or find a way to put them to one side.

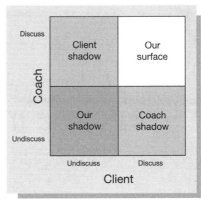

Shadow map

She decided to adopt a 'disclosure' approach for this as they had a high level of investment in the trust fund and she was sure that he would not share her confidences elsewhere. Julie talked about her experiences of making the big break. She described her journey and the role that the world travel played in giving her the confidence to dispel her limiting beliefs and make the foray into a new venture. She especially talked about some of the demons that stalked her (fear of no clients hence no revenue and hence no house). In talking about this she helped John to open up a bit more about his worries and doubts. For him the big concern was his children: how could he balance the two (seemingly) conflicting desires for freedom and security? He admitted that these demons attacked him every few days and that on more than one occasion he had nearly called Julie to cancel the programme.

As they both began to understand the deeper fears that were impacting his views of the change, they agreed that many of the fears were quite embedded and in many ways would cause more trouble to climb inside and eliminate. Instead they agreed to ensure that these concerns would be included in the criteria element of the Create stage to ensure that any potential solution would address them.

8

Create – find the best solution

The story so far

At this stage of the coaching partnership commitment has been established and both sides are confident in the chances of value being delivered. Building on this the coach has gained a greater insight into the person and their story. From this they have climbed deeper inside the picture painted by the client to unearth both the limiting beliefs and any internal brakes that might have been applied. Further to this they have addressed what (if any) shadow issues might exist and have been successful at turning those factors that the client felt were undiscussable into open issues they can comfortably share with the coach. As a result both coach and client are confident they now understand the whole story: what is really going on and what solutions need to be generated.

Enter the Create stage

This is where the coach and client work together to develop a solution that is robust and importantly deliverable. The first stage is to work together to identify a set of possible actions, then to ensure that the choice the client has made is a robust and sustainable one and not just a short-term fix that will be followed by reversion and disappointment.

Two models are considered in this stage. First, the CREATE model which seeks to overlay a structure and rigour behind the creative process. Second, the CHOICE framework, which tests the robustness of the final solution the client intends to take into the Change stage.

Create the solution

Imagination is the beginning of creation. You imagine what you desire, you will what you imagine and at last you create what you will.

George Bernard Shaw

At this stage the coach seeks to help the client move towards a position where they have a clear and robust set of solutions identified. The interesting thing about this stage is that there are many great books and theories on the issue of creativity and the generation of solutions, but at heart all these processes can be broken down into two very simple acts or questions:

▥ What could I do? A divergent process to create options.

▥ What should I do? A convergent process to select the optimum choice.

Think about the last car or flat you bought, or career change. No matter how you managed the process of identifying what solutions you would run with, all your actions revolved around these two processes: the divergent process (which could I do to resolve this problem?) and the convergent process (which of the options should I choose?). These two core activities can be seen in Figure 8.1 where the client begins with no solution; ideas are generated using the divergent process; then the client selects from this list of ideas to pursue the solution that seems most favourable (convergent process).

Examples of this can be seen on the popular TV shows where people want a serious life change and believe that the answer is a place in the sun: a villa in Spain or a beach-front hut in Goa. The same process can be seen as the

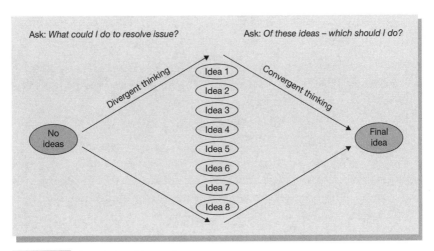

Figure 8.1   Could–should questions

TV host discusses the couple's needs; presents where they could move to and what they could buy; then the participants consider which they should buy and in some cases do!

However, if it were that simple the coach would have very little to do and the client could wander off, find their solution and come back to present it to the coach all wrapped and ready. The problem is that these two simple processes of 'could' and 'should' thinking often sound easier than they are. Instead of a smooth problem-solving process, most people follow a creative path that is hindered and harmed by biased mental process, comfort-zone thinking and often sheer laziness. In effect people often do what they have always done and therefore get what they have always got. So the Create stage becomes less creative and more conformist.

This is because when people are developing solutions to problems, the solutions have to come from somewhere. This 'somewhere' is often a residual databank of personal knowledge and experience. Although people can step outside this world and explore options and solution that others have developed, the human approach tends to follow the 'not invented here syndrome' and so people feel safer with solutions they know or have experienced.

> **❝ The human approach tends to follow the 'not invented here syndrome'. ❞**

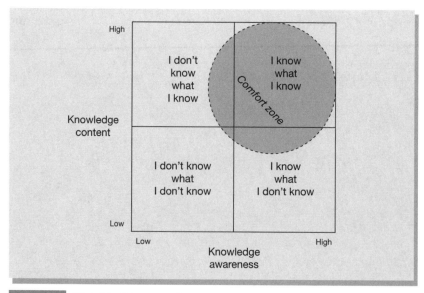

Figure 8.2 Know/don't know model

As we explore this idea it is useful to understand the simple model shown in Figure 8.2. With this we try to understand the client view using two questions:

■ Knowledge content: What is the knowledge bank they will draw upon? What explicit and tacit knowledge resides in the knowledge bank?

■ Knowledge awareness: To what extent are they conscious of their knowledge bank?

As we begin to understand the client's map it becomes possible to see four types of storage banks:

■ **I know what I know:** Imagine Jane, a management trainee who has just been on her first course and now understands the core management theories of motivation, communication and delegation. She is clear about the models and has a framework to deploy them.

■ **I know what I don't know:** However, she is also aware that some people on the course had some management training before joining the company and she was interested in the things that they knew that were not covered on the course. With this she is aware of the fact that there are areas of knowledge that she doesn't know but would like to.

■ **I don't know what I know:** Interestingly, Jane is also a part-time leader in an adventure group that takes children on trips to the Lakes. As part of this she has to deal with unruly and difficult children in what can be life-threatening situations. She makes no connection between this and her work and doesn't realize that much of what her colleagues on the management course know is simply what she does already as a team leader in her spare time. With this the capability is in her but she doesn't know it.

■ **I don't know what I don't know:** This is the deep treasure trove of potential that often lays untapped. Jack Dee the comedian sums this up nicely when he says, 'Real change comes from within the individual. The trouble is that the engine of that change is by no means evident to most of us, and thus we languish largely unfulfilled.'[1] This is the fact that people always have potential but this is overridden by the generation of solutions based on what they can actually do. Again this is often so self-evident in the television programmes where people take on new and alien roles in life, only to find that they can tap into an unrealized depth and transform themselves.

1 *The Times T2* (2004) Interview with Jack Dee, 17 Feb., page 9.

The problem is that people often tend to prefer to stay in the grey shaded area on the diagram and hence the solutions are a rehash of old ideas dressed up in a new way. So the phrase comes to mind that if you do what you always did, then you get what you always got. It is this inability or unwillingness to really look for solutions that are outside the comfort zone that can limit the chances of creating a solution that really helps the client to move forward. As a result the 'could' and 'should' diagram shown earlier ends up looking like the one in Figure 8.3. The limiting processes have reduced the number of ideas put forward because everything comes from the safety of the comfort zones.

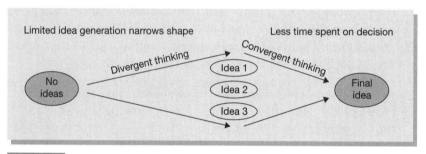

Figure 8.3 Restricted coulds and shoulds

The coach's primary job in the Create stage of the coaching process is to try to challenge any self-limiting beliefs and help the client to broaden the solution base. The goal will always be to help the client think the unthinkable and find innovative thoughts and ideas that they would have considered in isolation. In essence the goal is to widen the output side of the divergent (could) stage and to lengthen the time spent on the convergent (should) stage to ensure that the decision-making process is robust and people don't just select their old-time favourite idea, as seen in Figure 8.4.

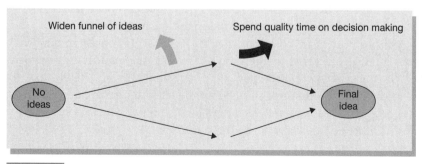

Figure 8.4 Could and should action

Where the coach fails to help the client both expand their potential solutions and carefully manage how they select their final solution, they are contributing to the delivery of a potentially successful but not very original outcome. If the client has not been pushed in these two areas, in many ways they could probably have done this on their own – so what is the value being added by the coach?

The CREATE process

Think about someone purchasing a new car. In a short space of time they will go through a complex decision-making process to choose the right one. However, this is something we often do intuitively and without any awareness of the strategies being followed. So, what steps do people actually follow?

The first stage is to have a clear understanding of the challenge: namely to set out the criteria that the car needs to meet. The second stage is to look for somewhere to buy the car. Once the dealers are identified the person might start to explore the different cars that are available. Once the options are understood, they move from an exploratory process to a decision-making approach. They might look at each of the cars in more detail and appraise them for suitability against the original criteria. As they go through this process, they will be testing each car against a set of criteria that probably includes cost, quality and reputation. Finally, they will prioritize and evaluate the options to make the final choice. This process might take an hour or it might be over in the blink of an eye. However long, the goal is to follow a journey that takes you first down the divergent path of thinking, closely followed by a style of thinking that is convergent in nature as seen in Figure 8.5.

> **❝ The first stage is to have a clear understanding of the challenge. ❞**

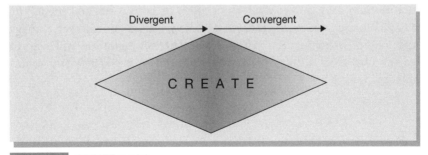

Figure 8.5   CREATE model

The divergent (or, what could I do?) stage of the journey will be driven by three attributes:

- **Challenge:** The need to define clearly the criteria being used to assess the outcome, i.e. what good will look like.

- **Randomize:** Then brainstorming potential solutions, a deliberate process to generate a rich tapestry of options.

- **Explore:** Finally, consider playing with each of the ideas to understand the strengths and weaknesses.

The underlying aim at this stage is to avoid any form of judgement or criticism. It is essential that you do not allow the client to slip into creative laziness where a judgemental hat is worn as soon as the ideas start to roll. However, once the idea-generation phase is complete, the next stage is to shift into a convergent style of thinking, where the client can take a more critical role of the ideas they have put forward.

The convergent (or, what should I do?) process is used to bring the client from a divergent state into that of critic or judge of the ideas generated. This process will typically draw upon three styles of thought:

- **Appraise:** Assess each one and filter out those that intuitively do not help resolve the original issue.

- **Test:** Validate the remaining ideas against the criteria set out in the challenge stage at the outset of the process.

- **Evaluate:** Finally, prioritize each of the remaining options against the core requirement to ensure that the end solution deals with the problem.

The client might understand that by using such a tight framework there is a chance they could feel restricted or unable to be really 'creative'. Although these arguments are valid, experience suggests that creativity must be managed and cannot be left to chance. As such it can help to use a process that is simple, logical and easily understood by both coach and client. The CREATE model, outlined in more detail below, isn't the only way to manage the solution stage of the coaching cycle but its application will help to ensure that ideas are originated and deployed in a practical and robust manner.

Challenge

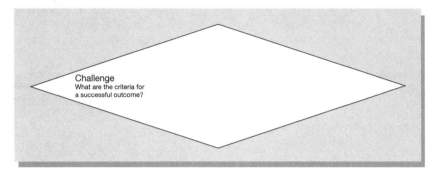

Figure 8.6   The challenge stage

The first stage of the divergent process is to ensure that the criteria for success are clearly established. Wherever possible, try to get the client to put a clear objective for the creative challenge in writing. Develop a clear and succinct statement that sets out what you hope to achieve at the end of the Create stage of the coaching process. This statement will indicate the problem (as defined in the Client or Clarify stage) and the criteria that the end solution will meet. As mentioned, that will often be based around time (by when), cost (how much can be spent) and quality (how good it has to be). But other criteria can be used, such as people to be involved or not involved, or what the client doesn't want to give up (such as family commitments). The key is to set out a tight set of criteria that will help make the final decision in the convergent phase of the Create process.

Imagine someone who is looking to make a major career change and is struggling to find any clear direction or way forward. Before the coach and client rush to a solution, they both need to be clear as to any defined boundaries or criteria that will indicate a successful solution, These criteria questions might be:

▪ What are the criteria for a good solution?

▪ When does the solution need to be in place?

▪ Is there anything out of bounds?

▪ How would they know a good solution if they saw it?

▪ What are the cost limitations?

▪ How much can they spend on achieving the change?

▪ What are the quality criteria? How perfect does the solution have to be?

By ensuring that the challenge is clearly set out in the convergent stage, the final solutions can be tested against a clear and defined set of criteria.

Randomize

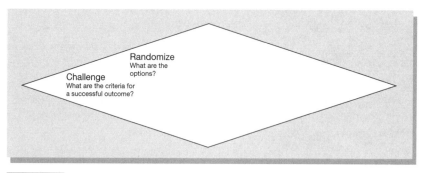

Figure 8.7 The randomize stage

If we are going to originate new ways of thinking, it is important to step outside the box – to take on board new and chaotic ways of viewing the world. This randomization of potential solutions can help to push back the boundaries and take on a new perspective. Leonardo da Vinci believed that to gain knowledge about the form of a problem you had to look at it from different perspectives. He felt that by simply sticking to the first view, you would be left with a limited impression of what the object was and what it might be.

> **If we are going to originate new ways of thinking, it is important to step outside the box.**

However, helping people to step outside their normal frame of reference is difficult, as they need to let go of their comfortable thinking styles and practices. One way to achieve this is to use different techniques that force the mind to operate in areas of uncertainty:

- **Randomize:** Take an encyclopedia or dictionary and pick random words. Use these to stimulate new ideas and actions associated with the engagement. Don't try to force anything, just let the back-of-the-mind thoughts trickle through to help originate new ways of working.

- **Connections:** Consider the change process and then link it with another idea. Help the client to imagine how the change process might operate like a town-centre tram or how they might use the caves in Spain as a training location.

■ **Opposites:** If you think of many of the new ideas that surface, they are actually the opposite of what is traditionally being used: the shift from fixed phones to mobile phones; private rather than public investment in the transport infrastructure; or disposable rather than long-lasting razors.

■ **Explode:** Take one idea and then grow it, like an expanding balloon – see where it goes when self-imposed limits are taken away.

■ **Reframe:** Take the client topic and reframe from a problem to a golden opportunity. Imagine that what is being offered is actually the solution required and then work through how such an opportunity is used. Alternatively, take the issue and turn it into a negative. If the topic is how to lose weight, turn it round and see weight gain as a valuable opportunity. See what ideas this type of reorientation produces.

■ **Why, why:** Take one of the issues or options and repeatedly ask why. Force people to dig deeper and deeper into the problem so that new and more divergent solutions are created. This can also be used in a revolutionary mode to encourage the client to break their tacit rules of thumb, especially if they can't remember why those particular rules were instituted in the first place.

■ **Reminiscing:** Encourage people to use 'this reminds me of . . .' statements in relation to aspects of the change process. This uses the power of recall to stimulate people to make links with other experiences.

In trying to originate new ideas, the danger is that both you and the client will sit in the comfort zone, offering ideas that don't step outside the safe domain. However, this is where the role of the coach comes in – to push and nudge the client to stretch their thinking and really consider what they might do to help resolve their situation.

Beware at this stage the enthusiasm and passion of the coach overstepping the ethical and professional boundary. It is at this point that many coaches think their role is to also input ideas so that they can 'help' the client. While this might be nice help in the short term, especially when the client is stuck, the difficulty is that it can create more long-term problems for the following reasons:

■ **Power wrapper:** Each little nugget of an idea the coach offers up is surrounded in a political wrapper. Underneath all coach/client relationships will be an inherent power relationship. The coach will nearly always be perceived as more powerful and with greater knowledge – hence anything they say must obviously be right. As a consequence the client accepts the coach's solution and negates the value of their own contributions.

- **Contextual fit:** Even where the coach does have prior knowledge, it is their knowledge from their context and it might not be appropriate for the client's world.

- **Temporal fit:** The fact that the coach may have prior knowledge is just that: prior. It may not be current and appropriate on a temporal basis. With the rate of change in society, organization knowledge is often out of date within months or weeks. In the coach's mind it may be current and in vogue but the reality might be that it has passed its sell-by date.

- **Dependency:** The moment the coach offers a solution, they are creating implicit dependency. If the client walks away thinking that they cannot solve their own problems, they will end up returning to the coach to solve the next problem. This can in many ways be viewed as a failed coaching engagement.

- **Blame game:** If the solution turns out to be a bad one then the client can blame the coach for it and minimize any error on their own part.

It is for these reasons that I believe that the coach should (wherever possible) seek to ensure that ideas emanate from within the client. If the client doesn't have the experience to originate the ideas then the coach's role is to help them find ways to dig out the solution. Maybe use the Internet, talk to other people, make a few mistakes and see what comes out. Whatever the process, the moment the coach steps into the role of content provider they face the risk of being part of the problem and once this happens, all sense of objectivity, reason and independence will be slowly eliminated. If you don't believe me, try teaching your partner or child to drive – the idea may be great but the coaching or teaching process is inherently wrapped in the other aspect of the relationship and this can end up making the coaching process personal. It is this emotional involvement that can cause major problems in this randomize phase and is a critical point to beware of.

Explore

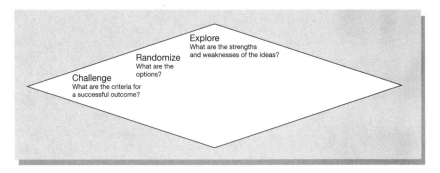

Figure 8.8   **The explore stage**

Once the ideas and potential solutions are generated, it is important to play with them and start to flesh out how they might be used. This means that each of the ideas is played with in the same way that a baby experiments with a new toy. Question the purpose of the idea, see how it might be used and find out what practical value it holds. Try to put some flesh on each of the ideas that emerges from the randomize stage and really understand how they might be applied in a practical way. While the randomization stage is 90 per cent idea and thought based, the exploring stage is 90 per cent hard effort – actually taking the wild ideas and really trying to understand how they might contribute to the problem at hand. You can achieve this by asking the following types of questions:

■ How would it work?

■ What are its strengths?

■ What are the potential problems with it?

■ Can it be used in any other way?

■ What happens if it is used with another option?

■ How would it be organized?

■ What resources would it need?

■ Where are the synergies?

The exploring stage is the final element in the divergent process. From this point onwards the goal is to reduce the number of ideas. Hence it is important to ensure that all of the ideas are really pushed to their limits to understand what value they might add.

Appraise

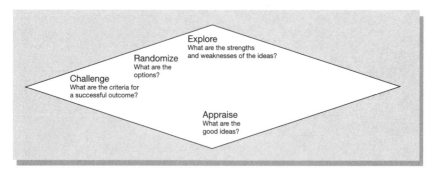

Figure 8.9   The appraise stage

Building on the toy metaphor, when a child is faced with a floor full of toys it will naturally start to appraise which of them to play with. In the Create model, the appraisal stage is used to make the transition from divergent to convergent thought patterns and so start the closure phase. The coach's role at this stage is to help the client 'intuitively' filter out those ideas that do not seem to add value or are less effective than others offered in the generative stage. Although this stage will often be instinctive rather than explicit, you must ensure that intuitive disposal is not used as an excuse to get rid of those ideas that are too risky or step outside of the normal mode of operation. If the client seeks to reject an idea, then test to ensure that it really is not feasible and is not just a case of them being scared because it sits outside their normal area of experience.

> **The coach's role at this stage is to help the client 'intuitively' filter out those ideas that do not seem to add value.**

The basic process is to take all the ideas that have been generated as part of the randomization and exploring stages and subject them to a first pass of rejection. Using both intuitive and explicit knowledge and experience, take a first pass at all the ideas and weed out those that seem totally unpractical. One way to do this is to write all of the suggestions on paper and spread them over a wall or floor. Ask the client to go through the list and mark those that they totally reject, are not sure about, and really favour as having potential. It is then possible to discard those that have been rejected as unsuitable and focus on the ones that the client believes might add value. It is important to point out that those ideas in the possibility pile should not be pushed aside in favour of those that have full backing from the client. At some point it is important to test these ideas. But where time is of the essence, this quick appraisal process can highlight the ideas to be focused on initially.

Test

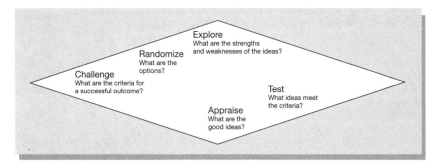

Figure 8.10   The test stage

Once the intuitive appraisal process is complete, the coach will need to help the client be more explicit and rigorous in selecting the ideas that will be put forward. This is the final stage the ideas pass through to ensure they offer effective solutions. Although this might be undertaken in many ways, one of the more effective approaches is to use a criteria-based selection model. At the very outset of the exercise, you can determine the criteria that any final solution must meet to ensure that an effective outcome is achieved. The criteria used in this stage will be the standards set in the Challenge stage of the Create process. In this sense it is quite simple – either an idea meets the criteria agreed up front or if it fails to meet the standard it is put to one side. Although it may be revisited later, in the short term it is best to focus on those that meet the criteria, otherwise the client will end up with solution drift.

Evaluate

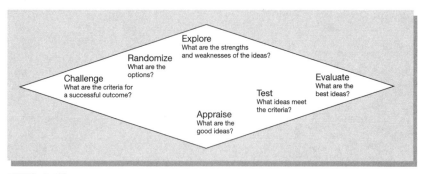

Figure 8.11 The evaluate stage

Finally, once the number of potential solutions is down to a short list, they can be evaluated against the core challenge set out at the start of the Create process. At this stage it is important to ensure that emotion does not creep into the decision process. Although emotions are critical throughout the creation process, at this stage they become dangerous. If the client is allowed to push their personal favourite then the creative rigour of this model can be compromised.

Managed CREATE

One of the most important objectives in any coaching engagement is the drive to create a solution that is both innovative and practical. It is essential to ensure that the full creative processes are stimulated but with the caveat that the client's solution can be delivered within the given constraints. To achieve this delicate balance it is important to ensure that managed creativity rather than freewheeling creativity is adopted.

The end result is that the client has been helped through a structured process that tackles a number of issues, but in essence deals with the two core problems of creativity raised at the outset. First, it pushes them to move outside their bounded reality and develop ideas and solutions that they might not normally have considered. Second, it encourages them to adopt a rigorous approach to the idea selection process and hopefully avoid the common problem of 'I will pick this because I like it'. Rather, they can say why they are opting for a particular solution and what describes the rationale behind their selection. This process can be seen as the CREATE model, shown in Figure 8.12.

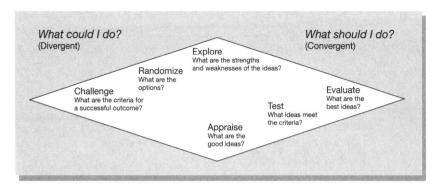

What could I do?
(Divergent)

Explore
What are the strengths
and weaknesses of the ideas?

Randomize
What are the
options?

Challenge
What are the criteria for
a successful outcome?

Test
What ideas meet
the criteria?

Appraise
What are the
good ideas?

What should I do?
(Convergent)

Evaluate
What are the
best ideas?

Figure 8.12   **CREATE framework**

The coach has an interesting role in all this. At the 'could' stage their role is to mercilessly push the client to expand their cognitive and emotional processes, to really tap into the unknown possibilities and explore ideas they might not have considered before. This is also guaranteed to irritate the client as they will feel bullied and under pressure to stretch a muscle that is rarely used. On the downside the coach is again mercilessly challenging the client to present the logic of a decision. Why is one choice better than another? And it is not good enough to say 'because it is!'. If we are to help ensure that the final solution is considered and robust then we need to challenge times when the emotional heart kicks in and takes over the choice-making process.

To do the job properly the coach will be challenging deep emotional, cognitive and behavioural habits. Hence it is really important at this stage to share the CREATE framework with the client prior to embarking on the solution stage. This way they will understand why you might appear to be obstructive and overly critical. In addition, by understanding the deeper aspect of a good creative process it enables the transfer of responsibility to the client for the outcome and minimizes the risk of solution dependency.

Coaching questions

Challenge
▪ What are the criteria for a good solution?
▪ When do you need them by?
▪ Is there anything out of bounds?
▪ How would you know a good solution if you saw it?
▪ What are the cost limitations?

	▓ How much can you spend?
	▓ What are the quality criteria? How perfect does the solution have to be?
Randomize	▓ What could you do?
	▓ What mustn't you do? What is the opposite of that?
	▓ What is the most outrageous thing you could do?
	▓ What would the person you most admire do?
	▓ What would the person you least admire do?
	▓ What would the prime minister suggest?
Explore	▓ What are the strengths of each option?
	▓ What are the weaknesses of each one?
	▓ What are the costs of each one?
	▓ What are the consequences of each one?
Appraise	▓ Which of these seems to be a good idea?
	▓ Intuitively would you keep it in?
Test	▓ Does it meet the criteria set in the Challenge stage?
	▓ How can you be sure that it meets the criteria?
	▓ How can you be sure that it doesn't meet the criteria?
Evaluate	▓ Which is the best idea?
	▓ How would you rank the others?
	▓ What is the worst idea? Why?
	▓ Which will you take forward?

Choose the choice

It's choice, not chance, that determines your destiny.

Jean Nidetch

Once the client has defined their preferred solution, it is easy to fall into the trap of the euphoric moment when everyone is gung-ho and ready for action. This might be the person who has decided that doing an Open University course will help with their promotion; the client who believes that their fear of presenting will be addressed by attending stage school; or the person who believes that their problem with hitting their best marathon time can be solved by undertaking more winter training.

At this stage the coach's role is to again slow down the process for a second by pushing the pause button. They need to challenge the client to test the choice is the optimum one. It is easy to make a choice that is right but doesn't last or the choice that is wrong but lasts. The difficulty can come in being sure that the choice is the optimum one and will stand the test of time.

There are many factors that help determine what makes the difference between a good or bad choice but often it comes down to the rigour of the selection at the end of the Create stage. The challenge is when the client picks their final proposal from the list of evaluated options can they be sure that it is the optimum choice? It may look the best on paper, but when trying to deliver a sustainable outcome in a live situation, will they really go through with the pain of change and will it hold up to scrutiny by the commercial or social market?

There are six factors that when fully evaluated and understood can have a significant impact on the long-term success of a client's choice. These factors are shown in Figure 8.13.

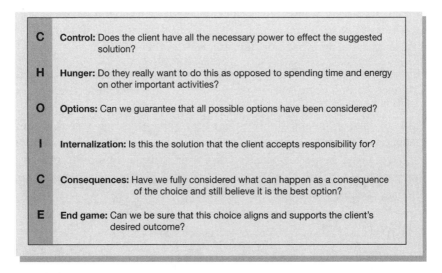

C **Control:** Does the client have all the necessary power to effect the suggested solution?

H **Hunger:** Do they really want to do this as opposed to spending time and energy on other important activities?

O **Options:** Can we guarantee that all possible options have been considered?

I **Internalization:** Is this the solution that the client accepts responsibility for?

C **Consequences:** Have we fully considered what can happen as a consequence of the choice and still believe it is the best option?

E **End game:** Can we be sure that this choice aligns and supports the client's desired outcome?

Figure 8.13 Factors impacting on the long-term success of a client's choice

> **❝ Managing these six factors doesn't guarantee that the solution will be successful. ❞**

Managing these six factors doesn't guarantee that the solution will be successful. What it does do is help the client become more conscious of the factors that affect their chances of achieving sustainable success.

Control over outcome

Question: Does the client have all the necessary power to deliver the suggested solution?

The coach should test the client to see whether they are making a choice about something where they have control or whether they are simply spending time and energy on something that is outside their area of influence.

Consider the client who comes to the coach with an issue at work. They are having a problem with their boss who always seems to be picking on them. This has led to an unhealthy environment that is creating stress for the client and tension for others in the office. However, in the coaching session the client always wants to focus on the boss and how if only they would change what they did then things would be sorted. In many ways this is like someone who sits on the outer ring of a children's roundabout wheel and spends all their time moaning about how sick they feel. They have a choice: stay there or move to the inner part of the wheel where the centrifugal force will stop acting and they can relax and watch others feel sick.

It is far more productive to help the client move into the centre of the roundabout and focus energy on things that are under their immediate control and can be resolved by them without recourse to anyone else. So with the person moaning about their boss, they need to realize that they can't change their boss's behaviour. That is not under their control and is unlikely to ever be the case. Instead they need to move from the 'Can't' ring on the wheel into the 'Can' and try to focus their energy on what they can change to make a difference (Figure 8.14).

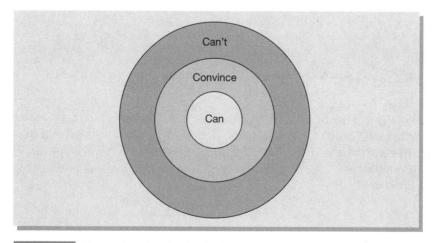

Figure 8.14   The can/convince/can't wheel

The great thing is that the more the client chooses their choices and deals with issues that impact the inner circle, the more chance there is to make a choice that is successful. Consequently the client's 'Can' circle becomes wider and the 'Can't' circle shrinks. The result is that their personal power grows proportionally.

The third area in the choice circle is the Convince area. This sits between the 'Can' and 'Can't' wheels. It offers a solution when the client wants to make a choice but they don't have direct control over the situation. In this case it might make sense to focus on either convincing others to help them achieve the outcome or on tackling those people directly to convince them to change.

Ultimately the coach has to help the client realize that there are three types of choice: the choice where you can deliver the intended outcome; the choice where they would like to but can't actually deliver the intended outcome; and the choice where they need to convince others to support their goal. The great coach helps the client spend time in the area that will realize the most payback. More importantly, if they see that the choice made at the end of the CREATE model is one that the client cannot actually deliver, they should challenge them to really question the wisdom of taking such action.

Hungry for success

Question: Will the client really want to do this rather than spend time and energy on other activities?

This stage attempts to understand the emotional content of the choice and gauge the client's passion or motivation behind the decision. An intelligent choice made without the emotional quotient may be brilliant, but is unlikely to be either sustainable or successful.

Diets don't work. This is an often-quoted maxim but generally with good cause. The reasons why they don't work are many, but one of the factors that can cause them to fail (in the long term, if not in the short term) is the fact that people don't really want to lose weight. They say they do, the telly says they should, the magazines suggest that it is great to be a size eight, but the fact of the matter is that it isn't really something they deep down want to achieve. They say they do – but not enough to give up the late night chocolate bar or get up for the early morning jog.

If you do something you don't particularly want to do now, then at some point later the urge will come to do the things that you really want to do.

This happens with so many people who take up careers, hobbies and other activities because of peer pressure or short-term knee-jerk reaction. Because their heart isn't really in the choice, at some point later they change direction or terminate the journey totally.

Even though the client knows what they want to do and how to get there, this is generally not enough. They need passion and perseverance. It is this emotional self-direction needed to manage and overcome the problems and obstacles that will surface after the choice is made. Take any client who set out a clear and focused action place for making a change in their life. It is rarely the choice of what to include in the action plan that makes the final difference. In most cases it is the passion they wrap around the choice. For someone who is about to diet, selecting the dietary process is simple: the difficulty comes two or three weeks into the process when it is their best friend's birthday party. Can they really say no to the cake or the glass of champagne? It is at this point that the direction and energy provided by the emotions need to kick in and provide the strength to say no. Without this support, any choice will be short-lived.

As coaches we need to really challenge and press the client to ensure that the passion exists and that they are really hungry for the change to the exclusion of all distractions that will surface. We must test whether the client is prepared to fight for the right to make their change stick. Hunger leads to desire, desire leads to dreams and dreams lead to passion and committed action. Where the coach senses that there is little or no passion or hunger for the change, the chances are that it will be a non-sustainable outcome.

Options for action

Question: Can you be sure that all possible options have been considered?

This stage of the CHOICE model is the head or logical part of the equation. It provides the final wisdom and clarity of purpose that can regulate the excesses of an emotional heart. The heart says, 'I know where I'm going and I'm going to get there by hook or by crook.' The head says, 'Fine, but let's make sure we actually make it in one piece so it's a really effective journey.' To do this the head needs to have breadth of choice. It needs to be able to call on a range of views and ideas to ensure the direction set by the heart is achieved, though it won't necessarily be by the route the heart had envisaged.

The trouble is that we often restrict our options for choice without consciously realizing it. This occurs for a number of reasons, including:

■ **Dead choices:** Sometimes people act as though the commitment they made with a previous choice means that they have to keep going down the same route. When this happens we can fall into the trap of religiously following 'dead' choices. People want to believe they are good at making choices and so persist in convincing themselves that the original decision was a good one, even when it appears not to be. As a coach I sometimes see this when people have invested so much time and energy in a relationship that they're loath to let it go, even when it is clearly a destructive influence on their life. Clients will often have a serious emotional investment in things that are part of their life and getting rid of them would be like saying that the earlier choices were bad. Part of the coaching role is to help them accept that choices made in the past might be lost and can't be recovered. Once made they are dead and gone and the coach must help the client focus on the rationality of the choices to be made in the future rather than those made previously.

■ **Discounting:** People set their own discounting rules. Research suggests that young children faced with a choice between getting an attractive toy in five minutes or a less attractive toy immediately will choose the latter. We can all become temporarily myopic and just focus on those options that give the earliest payback. This is clearly impulsiveness and can often be seen in problem-solving situations where the tendency is to respond quickly with a solution rather than waiting to get one that offers a better outcome. By doing this we are discounting the value of the future option. This is because we believe that by taking the sooner option we start to accumulate interest (in the form of benefit) through use of the choice now rather than later. This can restrict variety because we ignore possible choices that do not deliver an 'immediate' benefit. The clearest example of this can be the depletion of fish stocks, eradication of the forests or depletion of the world's natural energy sources.

The coach must help ensure they have helped the client to develop sufficient options to deliver the required solution. This is often known as Ashby's law of requisite variety. Ashby suggested that any regulator must have as much or more variety than the system it regulates. In a game of chess, the variety of moves or options you have available must be greater than the variety of moves available to your opponent. The same can be seen in football, the stock market, a children's painting competition. In any situation, you have to understand how much choice and variety exist, and then be able to match or exceed this level. The person with the most options and flexibility will lead the pack.

> **❝ Has your client truly considered all the possible options in resolving their solution. ❞**

The question is, has your client truly considered all the possible options in resolving their solution or have they knowingly or unknowingly restricted the level of variety in their system?

Internalization of responsibility

Question: Does the client take full responsibility for the consequences?

It is important to understand whether the solution the client has chosen is intentional or imposed. Is it one that other people or circumstances have forced on the client or is it one they choose to make? This is often referred to as the locus of control. Locus is a fancy word for location. It refers to where the client believes the controlling elements of the choice are coming from. Do they believe that it is being driven by an external circumstance, or do they believe that it comes from within them and that they determine the course of their life?

People who internalize operate from a self-concept that says, 'I take responsibility for both good and bad things that happen in my life.' People who externalize take the view that 'I can't take responsibility for the good or bad outcomes because they stem from the action taken by other people'.

Most of us fall somewhere in the middle, believing that the life we have is a combination of our own effort and outside circumstances that affect the outcomes of events in our lives. So at times we are under the pressure of others and sometimes life is under our control.

For example, I often come across people who have a very external locus of control because they believe that it is the company's responsibility to train and educate them. Because they put the responsibility for their learning on the manager or company, they have abdicated responsibility for both the direction and the outcome of any development. As a consequence they learn under sufferance and blame the company when they don't have the skills that are necessary to service once the market has changed.

The problem is that once people fail to take ownership of the problem they face, they will not seek to deliver a sustainable outcome. People who have an internal locus of control ('internalizers') think that they are responsible for their successes and failures. They believe that if they succeed it is because they try hard and have the ability to succeed. Other people may feel they do not have control over what happens to them. If good things happen it is due to luck, circumstances or other people. These people have an external locus of control ('externalizers').

The coach must listen carefully to the client's speech patterns to identify which position they are coming from:

Internal locus	External locus
I can control my feelings.	She made me so mad.
I was sick and chose to rest.	I couldn't do my homework.
I decided not to call you because . . .	I couldn't go to class.
I prefer or I chose . . .	I must . . .
I chose not to . . . because . . .	I can't . . .
I will get my degree.	If only I had my degree.

If the client believes they have control over future events, they will attempt to exert that control in order to achieve a positive outcome. It does not matter whether an outcome is or is not attainable, the perception of control determines whether one will try to attain it. For example, if Martin believes that by working on a project he will gain the visibility needed to get promotion, he will present a great image. The alternate mindset is to moan about being given yet another project and blaming the bosses for their failure to understand his potential for promotion.

If the client is externalizing the solution made in the CREATE stage and just doing it because they have to or because someone else says it must be done, the chances are that it will fail to deliver sustainable value.

Consequences understood

Question: Have I helped the client to fully consider what can happen as a consequence of the choice and do they still believe it is the best option?

As considered already, choices are crossing points in time. Each choice point is a branch on the tree, terminating in a list of consequences that follow if that branch is selected (Figure 8.15). Often these consequences lead to a new set of choices and resulting consequences. Every choice creates a new future and with this a set of (virtually infinite) consequences. But more importantly, choices represent or anticipate the future they are trying to create.

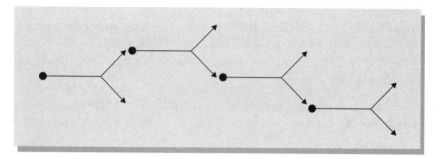

Figure 8.15   Choice chain

For each choice that you might make there will be a set of consequences. These will have a range of possible benefits and problems, but in simple terms we can assume that no matter what choice is taken, the consequences will fall into Highs and Lows (Figure 8.16).

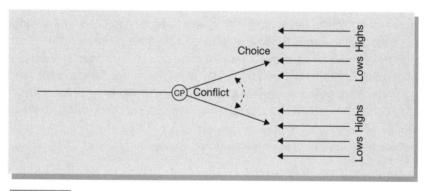

Figure 8.16   Highs and Lows

The Highs are those consequences that will give a positive return on the investment. These repay the time and energy invested and validate that the choice was the right one. The Lows are outcomes that offer less benefit and can actually act against the value of the choice, thus negating its primary value. It might be that there are so many Lows or one of the Lows has such intensity that it negates the choice made and a further choice might need to be taken to resolve the situation.

This is because every choice implies at least two options, each of which has positive and negative consequences. When choosing one option, you get its positive consequences and avoid the rejected option's negative consequences; but at the same time you must accept the chosen option's negative consequences and miss out on the rejected option's positive consequences.

Although the coach may try to help the client anticipate the future consequences when taking the choice, we can never know all possible implications of our choices; and even if we could, we wouldn't know which would come true. It is this uncertainty of the impact of each choice that leads to conflict in the decision-making process. These implications are in opposition with your natural goal to select good things and avoid bad things. Confusion can accompany your choice and can be felt even after you choose.

One way the coach can help the client is working with them to evaluate each option and map all its possible consequences. Once the possible Highs and Lows for each choice are understood, it becomes easier to take a stab at what choice will deliver the best sustainable success.

End game fit

Question: Can I be sure that this choice aligns and supports the desired outcome?

The coach must try to help the client to 'step into the future', to clearly understand their desired end game and ensure that the solution derived in the CREATE model will really take them in the right direction. Part of the role of the coach is to help the client consciously choose their choices and ensure that wherever possible they take them towards rather than away from their end goal.

> ❝ **The coach must try to help the client to 'step into the future'.** ❞

The key question you have to ask when helping the client make a choice is, do they have an end game to measure it against? If they don't have a clear outcome developed in the Client stage of the 7Cs, how can they know whether the choice they are about to make is moving them towards or away from the end point? The surest and most enticing way I can think to explain this is to use a quote from Lewis Carroll's *Alice's Adventures in Wonderland*:

> One day Alice came to a fork in the road and saw a Cheshire cat in a tree. 'Which road do I take?' she asked. 'Where do you want to go?' was his response. 'I don't know,' Alice answered. 'Then,' said the cat, 'it doesn't matter.'

Solution test

Once you understand the CHOICE model, it is relatively easy to apply these criteria to the solution that has been selected as the best option. The coach should encourage the client to pass the solution that emerges from the first part of the Create stage through the CHOICE model to assure its potential to deliver a sustainable value (Figure 8.17).

Control	The client does not have all the necessary control and power to deliver the desired outcome.	1 2 3 4 5	The client has all the powers required to deliver the desired outcome.
Hunger	The client is not passionate about taking the action.	1 2 3 4 5	They want to do this more than anything else at the time.
Options	This is the only option the client considered.	1 2 3 4 5	They have selected the action from a wide range of options.
Internalization	Someone or something else required them to take this action.	1 2 3 4 5	The client will take this action because they want to and not because of someone or something else.
Consequences	The client does not have a clear picture of what may happen.	1 2 3 4 5	They are clear as to all the possible consequences that might arise as a result of the action.
End game	The outcome will not take them towards where they want to be in the future.	1 2 3 4 5	They can describe how it will take them towards their end game.

Figure 8.17   The CHOICE model

As an example take the three CHOICE profiles shown in Figure 8.18. With profile (a) the problem might have been hunger and the solution is chocolate. While the first five parameters offer a high solution rating, the fact is that the whole end game (losing weight) has been discarded. This can happen in life where people panic after losing their job and take the first thing that comes along.

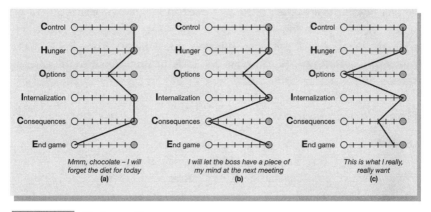

Figure 8.18 Choice profiles

With profile (b), all the parameters apart from consequences have been considered. This might be deemed as the 'knee-jerk' solution. This can be seen where clients jump for a solution because it meets what they want now but they fail to really think through the consequences of their action. It is this type of solution that often leads to problems when the client makes a choice like signing up for a degree course that will help with their promotion but without understanding the impact it will have on their personal finances for the next three years.

Profile (c) is a pattern that has been found time and time again as people see the latest sports car in the Sunday press. I did this when purchasing a motorbike. After passing my test the only answer to the question was a Harley Davidson. I didn't consider any other options even though this raised a number of specific consequences. I knew they were there, I just didn't want to look at anything else. This is the 'fad solution'. For example, yet another new book comes along espousing that people need to follow the path offered up by the latest guru, and people say, 'Yes that is the answer for me' and don't take the time to consider other options. If you look back over the past thirty years we can see wave after wave of personal development fads that enter mainstream thought, hang around for a while and then drift away as people being to realize that maybe it isn't quite the answer they believed it to be. The challenge for the coach is to always ask the question, 'And what else could you do?' Never accept an 'either – or' range of options. As a minimum there will always be a third option and in most cases a fourth, fifth, etc. Unless these are thoroughly tested in the Create stage, how can you and the client be sure that you have the 'optimum' rather than the 'only' solution?

As mentioned already, the CHOICE profile cannot guarantee that a solution will work and be sustainable. What it can do is to help understand the deeper dynamics of a potential solution that emerges from the CREATE model and acts as a checklist before you take the final step into the Change stage of the coaching framework.

Coaching questions

Control
- Is this under your control?
- Could anyone stop you from doing this?
- Could anything stop you from doing this?
- Would you have to convince anyone to make it happen?

Hunger
- How important is this?
- Why is it important?
- What would you give up to achieve it?
- What if you were told that you could not do it?

Options
- How many options did you think of?
- How many should you have thought of?
- Is there anything else you could have done to look for other possibilities?

Internalization
- Why are you doing this?
- Is it because you want to do it or you think someone else wants it to happen?
- What could stop you from doing it?
- Whose fault might it be if it doesn't work out?

Consequences
- What are the consequences of doing this?
- What are the costs?
- What are the highs?
- What are the lows?

End Game
- Does this take you towards your perfect picture?
- How does it do that?
- How do you know it takes you in the right direction?

John's journey

Julie now felt that she had a clear enough understanding of John's story to move into the Create stage and try to develop solutions that would help achieve his outcome. To help with this she took John through the CREATE tool. She did this first by tracing a number of creative processes that he had been involved with in the past few years and then

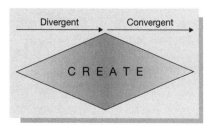

CREATE frame

demonstrating how these all fitted into the framework. Once she was sure that he understood the tool and its value she suggested he used it to develop a few ideas on what he could 'do' to help achieve his goal. They agreed that he would only complete the Challenge, Appraise and Explore section; they would then go through these at the next meeting and move into the Appraise, Test and Evaluation steps.

When John came back to the next meeting Julie praised the ideas he had developed, but then pushed him to develop another ten. At first John became angry and frustrated because he believed that he had exhausted the idea bank, but after pushing from Julie, he realized that the self-limiting beliefs discovered in the Clarify stage had come into play and internally he had restricted his willingness to be free with the idea generation and as a consequence came up with only fairly safe and predictable solutions.

With about 25 ideas listed, they then worked through these to pare down to the final top five ideas that John would take forward, with one of them being a definite that he would act upon immediately. In this stage Julie had to constantly challenge John with questions about why he was rejecting ideas and why one idea was better than another. This is because she wanted to be sure that John didn't just pick the old favourites and that he really worked through the selection process to come up with a solution that was robust and deliverable.

Once they had a range of solutions to take forward, Julie then asked John to do the Choice test on the primary solution. She really wanted to ground the idea and test that it was both a good idea and one that would be a robust choice that would deliver sustainable value.

In passing the top five ideas through the CHOICE model, one interesting outcome was that the top idea was not totally under John's control because others could have a major influence on its variability. But the second-choice solution came out with a robust score and importantly it was totally under John's control to achieve. Because of this they agreed to swap the first and second solutions in the prioritized list and that John would embark on action with the new first solution. The new second idea would be attempted once John had gained some confidence from acting upon the primary solution.

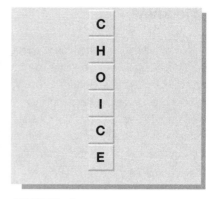

CHOICE test

John's primary solution was to search out and make contact with a wide (functional and geographic) range of personal trainers. The primary goal was to have a basic network of colleagues in place before he left his current position. With this action identified the next move was for them to explore the Change and understand how to help John mobilize the necessary action.

9

Change – mobilize action

The story so far

At this stage of the coaching partnership commitment has been established and both sides are confident of the chances of value being delivered. The coach understands both the person and the picture they have painted. This picture has been tested to ensure that the client is operating at fact rather than fantasy level and all the important issues have been surfaced. Following this clarity the client has used the CREATE tool to develop a series of potential solutions and then used the CHOICE model to validate which of these will deliver sustainable value.

Enter the Change stage

The Change stage is the stage where feeling and thought turn into behaviour. It is the time where the person who wants to run the marathon has to get up on a Sunday morning; it is the time where the team member has to deal with the abusive manager; and it is the point where the person who wants promotion signs up and attends the personal development programme. It is all about action. The first three stages of Client, Clarify and Create are in the main theoretical; the coach and client can happily chew the fat for days, weeks and even months, reflecting on the past, commenting on what is happening and talking about the grand dreams of tomorrow. But change is when things have to happen.

It might be that the client is looking forward to this stage. Maybe they look forward to getting up a 5am for a run, not eating chocolate bars or losing their evenings on a college course. Maybe. But in the main my experience is that this is when it becomes difficult and when the pain can often begin to kick in. This is the point where clients cancel appointments, find excuses not to do something, and conveniently forget to bring their action plan along to the meeting. It is funny how that old fence that has been sitting there ready to be taken down for the last three years all of a sudden seems such a critical job when other, more painful activities come along. All of a sudden we find distraction that 'legitimately' means that the client cannot do what they agreed to do at the last coaching session.

This is because change can be a painful process and people (generally) don't like it because of the associated pain. This might be Heart pain, with the emotional loss in letting go of something; the Head pain associated with having to think of things in a new way; or the Hand pain, with physically letting go of old habits or behaviours and finding new ways of doing things. For example, on a training course in most cases people will find a chair and stay there for the duration. This might be because it is close to the window, they are next to their friend, or they like to be near the flipchart to be able to read it. Although the reason might seem silly to the observer, to the delegate it can be quite critical and they will miss a tea break just to ensure they hold on to the preferred place.

> **Change can be a painful process and people (generally) don't like change because of the associated pain.**

In the Change stage the coach must help the client consider what pain or potential resistance will be associated with the change; what feelings, thoughts and behaviours they will have to dispose of; and how they can help them discover a new way of operating. In doing all this they need to understand what level of intervention they can make to effect sufficient mobilization. Should they support the client in making the change and offer emphatic backing or do they need to be a lot more proactive in making sure that the client does what they said they would do by taking a more forceful approach?

Manage the Y-Curve

Human beings, by changing the inner attitudes of their minds, can change the outer aspects of their lives.

William James

In any coaching assignment it is often best to assume that there will be some form of resistance to the proposed change. This might be the minor whinge about having to get up 30 minutes earlier or the full-blown sulk and refusal to take part in the exercise any more. By preparing for the resistance the coach can both be ready for the consequences of any refusal to accept a new way of working and ideally talk about the topic with the client before it surfaces.

The coach and client must respect the fact that resistance is natural. The client must not feel guilty for feelings, thoughts or behaviours that seem to go against their stated outcome. If anything they might possibly welcome this as it is a clear indication that they are in the territory of real change and not fiddling around the edge of transformation. This reaction that people experience when dealing with change can be mapped in the form of a Y-Curve. It seeks to show in a simple chart how people often pass through a number of common stages as they move from old feelings, thoughts and behaviours and embrace a new way of being.

Letting go

The Y-Curve consists of two distinct stages (that may overlap). The first stage is the 'letting go' or disposal stage, as seen in Figure 9.1. This is where people learn they will have to modify how they currently think, feel or behave and will be expected to adopt a new set of patterns. The second stage is the 'looking forward' phase when people can start to discover the new ways expected of them.

The disposal stage of the Y-Curve suggests that as people have to let go of the present, so the associated pain can cause a fall in personal performance. This might be seen in the way that someone who is trying to improve their time management skills may see a fall in performance as they struggle to

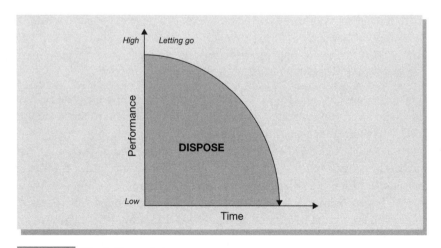

Figure 9.1   The 'letting go' phase

cope with the structure of a new system, or the addict goes through withdrawal symptoms as they work through the day-by-day process of retreating from the drug.

Often external events or stressors such as the death of a significant other, personal injury, illness, or change of residence will tend to force a person out of secure patterns. While the loss of a loved one through death or divorce is unquestionably shattering, humans mourn other losses as well: the end of a secure relationship, loss of a homeland, loss of a favourite job or even access to the local playing field to play soccer can be quite devastating for some people. Humans experience grief any time their life role is seriously changed and can be seen to move down the slope, with a consequential fall in personal performance.

However, the trigger for the disposal stage might not be just a negative driver. It might be a positive one. I know of many people who have been habitual smokers who have managed to give up in the blink of an eye simply because a child came into their life. They decided that life with the child in the house meant that they had to create a new way of living and found that this was enough to trigger a disposal of the habit. I spent many years (as a recovering alcoholic) trying to find a negative trigger to help me dispose of the old ways, but found that actually it was a positive-based one (I want to be successful) that really helped me turn the corner.

A key part of the disposal phase is often the need to let go. Part of this letting go might include an emotional release, a cognitive need to talk through things or even a behavioural response as people release pent-up anger or frustration. The coach should recognize such outbursts of anger as a natural part of the disposal process and possibly expect people to be selfish, childish and angry. They may well experience concern, denial, shock, worry and anger. This is the normal process and one that needs to be supported, surfaced and possibly talked about, not ignored.

Before people can adapt to and adopt new ways of thinking, feeling and behaving they must unlearn – to be able to let go of the emotional thoughts and behaviours that are of little further use. This is not the same as throwing away ideas. The brain doesn't erase feelings or memories, it changes the connections, renewing some, letting others fade away, under a form of selection. When we remember we recreate memories, based on those strengthened or weakened connections. In order to rebuild our cognitive maps and emotional memories, we have to throw away the old pattern.[1]

1 Battram, Arthur (1999) 10 December, http://world.std.com/-lo/96.09/0589.html.

However, simply letting go of things is not always as easy as it sounds. For example, the fact that knowledge is associated with power, prestige and political clout means that we are often loath to simply release it for others to use. In addition, unlearning is emotionally

ſſ Simply letting go of things is not always as easy as it sounds. 🥄

difficult because the old way of doing things has worked for a while and become embedded in our beliefs and behaviours.[2] We have to shift from the comfortable domain in the existing organizational environment and be prepared to migrate to the new form. This is based on the premise that we will be able to discard and forgo any existing mental models that might have held the status quo. This can be difficult because we often remain prisoners of our conceptual framework, where there is a general reluctance to leave the old way of thinking.[3]

Hence the act of disposal is critical to the change process but is rarely considered. The process of unlearning and how to help people discard redundant ideas and feelings is a crucial one that needs to be addressed as part of the coaching process. Unless we help the client learn how to let go of the past and redundant beliefs, they may find it difficult to accept and embrace new ways of working.

The coach should address a number of things in this stage by helping the client to understand the following:

▦ What else they are currently disposing or letting go of in their life.

▦ What they have disposed of in the past.

▦ How successful they have been at disposal.

▦ Where they have been successful at disposal what has helped to ease the process.

▦ Where they were not successful, what made it difficult.

▦ Whether association with certain people or things helped with the disposal process.

▦ How much time is a factor – do they typically have a long disposal cycle or can they typically let go of things really fast?

Once the client has been helped to understand how they typically dispose of redundant ways of feeling, thinking and behaving, then choices can be

2 Schein, Edgar H. (1993) 'How can organisations learn faster? The challenge of entering the green room', *Sloan Management Review*, Winter, page 87.
3 Nicolini, Meznar (1995) 'The social construction of organisational learning: conceptual and practical issues in the field', *Human Relations*, Vol. 48, No. 7.

made about their readiness to make the change. It might be that they are practised and accomplished in the art of disposal and so have little to worry about. Alternatively, it may be that they have regularly failed to make change because of the difficulty they have in letting go. Or it may be that there are certain things or contexts where they are able to let go, and other situations where it is more difficult.

One of the trends the coach might help the client to reflect on is their rate of dimensional disposal – to what extent they are able to let go of entrenched affective, cognitive and behavioural routines. Consider two aspects where someone is trying to dispose of the past and move on to a new way of operating:

■ **Divorce:** Clearly divorce is a painful process, and a key part of this pain arises from the disposal activity or letting go of the old ways. There is obviously no common way that people go through this disposal activity, but let's explore one person's journey. The divorce occurs amicably and the emotions have left without pain; behaviourally the couple don't see each other any more unless there is a need. However, there is this lingering problem of calling the new partner by the ex's name. The name is lodged in the brain and it can take months and for some people years to change the name association.

■ **Redundancy:** This is a change process that more and more people are experiencing and it can be a really interesting one. I know many people who have left the company emotionally and cognitively as soon as they are out of the door, but the funny thing is that they have this urge to revisit old haunts and meet with former colleagues. They will find reason to return and join in activities. So although they have discarded most of the past, there are behavioural hooks that exist.

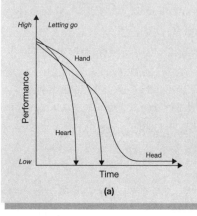

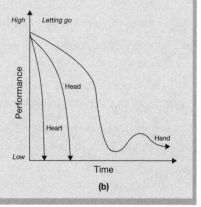

(a)   (b)

Figure 9.2 Letting go: divorce and redundancy

We could run the same mapping process with a host of other areas where people receive coaching. For example, smoking where people might find it difficult to dispose of the need to hold a cigarette (Hand), emigration and missing the emotional bond of friends and family (Heart). The coach's role is to help the client recognize that disposal or the ability to unlearn is a critical part of the process of learning. Once understood they should explore what their preferences might be and how these established patterns may impact the coaching topic.

An experience closer to home can be the agony involved in the transition to a new currency or metric system. This is simply because people know their imperial measurements so well that they will not and cannot forget them. This lock-in occurs because people like the old system, are proud of it and it comes easy. As a consequence many people still do (and will continue to) think using the non-metric system. For these people, letting go of the past is just too difficult or painful. The coach needs to ensure that the same doesn't happen for the client and that they are happy and ready to dispose of the old in readiness to accept the new.

Looking forward

Once people have been able to let go and dispose of the old ways of thinking and feeling, they can start to journey to discover the new ways expected of them. The discovery phase is the point when people will look forward in anticipation of what is to come.

Discovery is the process by which we acquire new ways of thinking, feeling and behaving. This might be through a range of processes, including reading, writing, conference presentations, working alongside someone, daydreaming, or working in a management team. The one thing they all have in common is the acquisition of knowledge.

The important point about the discovery phase is that people have to make a decision to let go of the past and move forward (Figure 9.3). Critically, this is a choice that must be made by the individual and not imposed by an outside agent. This might be an explicit decision in the form of a conscious choice to accept that they have to think, feel or behave in a new way. This might be someone who looks in the mirror and realizes that they really do need to get fitter, or the CEO who finally accepts that the current IT director is not up to scratch and they need to look for a new one. Or it might be a tacit decision – an emerging acceptance that things must change. This might be the realization that a couple come to when they accept that problems in their relationship need to be addressed. Critically it is the fact that the decision must be owned and internalized. Without this the change will be short-lived. For example, lots of people go on a training course – but few learn. So often they have been sent by the boss and did not make the personal choice to change. Without this conscious choice to change, little knowledge acquisition or change will occur.

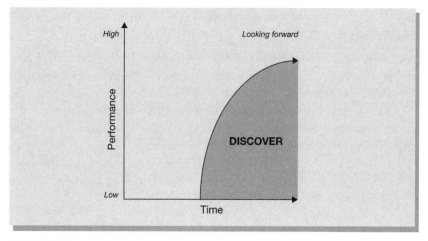

Figure 9.3 Looking forward phase

As with the disposal phase, discovery can take place across the three dimensions:

■ Heart – acquiring new ways of feeling about self and others and maybe new ways of expressing these feelings. This might be the person who suddenly discovers that they love a particular thing or person when for years they had no desire for it.

■ Head – developing new ways of thinking about self or the world. This might be new ideas, innovative thought patterns or simply new operating models. Examples might be new operating processes, slogans or heuristic patterns or rules of thumb that help make sense of the world. For example, how long does it take someone to adapt from looking one way at a junction when in their home country to reversing this when on holiday where people drive on the other side of the road? This is indicating their disposal rate of acquisition. When we go on holiday we know that my wife has to act as a second brain, giving me reminders to look certain ways until I have acquired the capability to reverse established driving patterns.

▪ Hand – where new behaviours or skills are gathered. One example for me was having to learn how to undo zips that clip on the other side of the jacket. When overseas I spent ten minutes looking extremely foolish in front of a sales assistant trying to undo a zip only to realize that it operated from a different side to that used in the UK. My intuitive motor reactions were to unclip the zip from one side, and even when I realized that it did the other way up, it took a while for my fingers to swap roles and so undo the zip.

For all of these the rate of discovery can vary (as seen in Figure 9.4). It can be rapid as when falling in love at first sight (Heart), experiencing a religious conversion (Head) or being able to naturally ride a bike or play an instrument (Hand). Conversely, the rate of discovery might be frustratingly slow. For me, no matter how hard I try I seem unable to learn how to wallpaper. I am not sure whether it is because I can't or just don't want to. But every time I try to wallpaper, no matter what I do bubbles appear and I just can't get them out. I am sure that I could learn to do this properly, but all the evidence (based on other experience) is that learning to gain new practical skills takes me a long while.

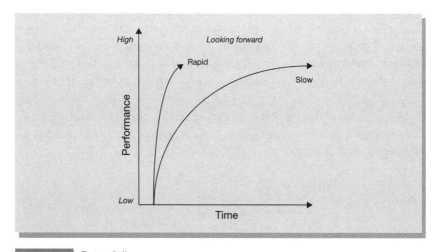

Figure 9.4 Rate of discovery

Some of the important areas and questions that the coach might explore with the client in relation to the discovery or acquisition of new ways of working include the following:

▪ Can you describe the top five ways that you use to discover new knowledge and ways of working?

- How would your friends or colleagues rate your ability to take on new ideas?

- Do you have a normal rate of acquisition for the Heart, Head and Hand capabilities?

- Is your preference to acquire tacit or explicit knowledge?

- Is there a demonstrated preference in terms of Heart, Head or Hand discovery?

- What was the last new way of working you acquired? Why was it successful?

- Do you like to discover new methods on your own or with other people?

- Who do you know is best at discovering new ways of working and what is it that they do to make them so effective?

It is important for the coach and client to understand the acquisition rate on a number of levels. First, it allows the coach to help tailor a change plan that fits with the established needs of the client and does not seek to pressure them into learning new ways too quickly. Second, it prevents frustration setting in when someone who has a shallow curve finds it difficult to take on board new ways of working. Third, it allows both coach and client to consider whether the curve rate might be tested as part of the coaching exercise – just because people 'typically' have a shallow curve (where it takes a while for them to adopt new ways of working) this doesn't mean that this norm cannot be challenged and changed.

> **66 It is important for the coach and client to understand the acquisition rate on a number of levels. 99**

Y-Curve

As we bring together the two stages of disposal and discovery we see the emergence of the Y-Curve. This is a representation of the pattern that people who have to go through a change process will tend to follow, as seen in Figure 9.5.

The important thing with the Y-Curve is the shaded area where the dispose and discover phases cross. This is the point where one of two things can happen. The first is people can go into the doldrums. This is a phase of just doing nothing – maybe the person who has lost their job and ends up sitting looking out of the window or watching daytime TV all day. People may tell

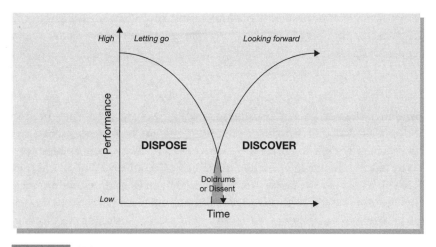

Figure 9.5   Y-Curve

them to 'snap out of it' but they get locked deep into this phase of nothingness. The idea of the Doldrums comes from the Lethargians, minute creatures in a book called *The Phantom Tollbooth* that live in perpetual boredom in the Doldrums. They change colours to match their surroundings and sometimes enforce laws against thinking and laughing. The key thing about the Lethargians is that they spend their life busily doing nothing.

The other reaction can be dissent. Whereas some people at the bottom of the Y-Curve will go into a malaise, others will get angry and seek to fight. They might attack the person or organization that pushed them into the bottom of the curve, or they may just lash out at the world around them. The target is often immaterial, it is just that fear or anger can emerge and needs to go somewhere. This is important for the coach to understand because in many cases the emotion might be aimed at them. This might result in tears, a verbal attack, not turning up to appointments or potentially a risk of physical action as people hit out at those closest to them when they are angry or stressed. The key thing for the coach to recognize at this stage is that it is not personal. At this point dissent can be the norm and the coach's role is to understand this and, more importantly, help the client develop strategies to manage this stage of the process.

In most cases 'resistance' simply means that some unconscious or shadow issues that affect someone's readiness to change haven't been met or surfaced. The approach of a good coach is to understand that the Y-Curve is a natural process for any change activity and then work with the client to help them create a solution that addresses all aspects. Having done this, the chances are that people will be ready and able to move up the discovery curve of the model.

The D-Spot

Although the next section considers many of the change strategies that can be employed to pull people out of the dip, the one consistent activity that will help anyone who enters the Y-Curve is to help them understand *why*. Why has the change happened? Why does it affect them? Why should they give up what they are doing? And why do they have to do something new in the future? Without the *why* factor people will often fail to step through the Y-Curve and simply revert to their old ways of thinking, feeling and behaving.

The critical point on the Y-Curve is the point where the dispose phase meets the discover phase. This is the D-Spot of the point where a conscious or unconscious decision needs to be made (Figure 9.6). This is the choice to move forward into the next stage or to reject the potential change and regress to the previous way of thinking and feeling.

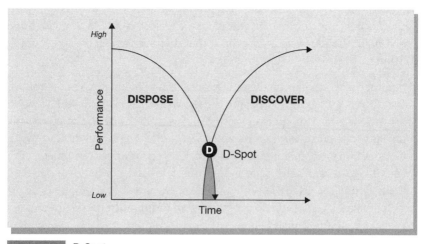

Figure 9.6 D-Spot

As people go down the disposal curve they will naturally get upset, angry and despondent. They will fall down the curve until they reach a point where they say enough is enough (either consciously or subconsciously). This is the point where one of three decisions can be taken (Figure 9.7). The first choice that people might make is to go back to point (1). In this case they will say this future position is not for me and refuse to go forward. This might happen when people consider taking redundancy with the goal of starting their own business but suddenly realize that this type of life is not as rosy as they first thought. Point (2) is where people hit the low point and don't come out. They might stay at this point, feeling angry and upset and as a consequence doing very little. Point (3) is where people choose to internalize the future and move out of the dip and into the new way of thinking, feeling and behaving.

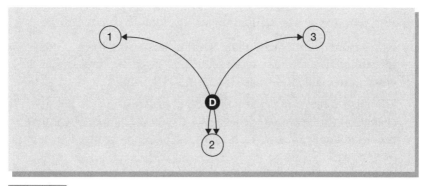

Figure 9.7 Three decisions

The important thing is that this is a choice, although not one that the client might be conscious of. The role of the coach is to manage the D-Spot and to help the client make a decision that will support the overall transformation they wish to achieve. The converse is that a failure to consciously address what choices people are likely to make at the D-Spot is what often leads to successful short-term change but failed long-term change.

Consider the example of someone breaking away from an employer to start out on their own. Over time the intent may grow and grow until this is a serious choice and one that starts to affect their commitment to the company they work with. This may not reflect itself in them doing a bad job, but their mental energies and enthusiasm may be channelled into other areas as they either consciously or subconsciously are disposing of the old emotional and cognitive link with the company.

In the end they start arriving at the D-Spot or zone of decision making. This zone is the most crucial. It is where they balance a range of things in their own mind. They know at this point that they can still abort the take-off. They can still get back on the corporate curve and get it back where it 'should have been' without anyone noticing. It is this decision zone that is the most important

❝ It is this decision zone that is the most important time. ❞

time. Many will put off the actual decision for as long as possible . . . just in case! The problem might be that at the very time they enter the 'zone' they become completely isolated. They may share their feelings with others in the corporation (or old way of life, whatever that may be). Many of these people will feel fear too – fear of losing a colleague/friend, fear that maybe they should be doing the same. There are no/few 'new friends' yet in the 'new way'.

This is often where the role of the coach needs to be considered. At the simplest level the coach can offer three contributions (Figure 9.8):

▨ Help ensure that momentum does not suffer or slow down as this is the point where stagnation can set in and the change process can slow down or in many cases stall.

▨ Minimize the level of pain that the client experiences as part of the change on the basis that the less pain, the more chance there is that people will not stop and revert to the old (and more comfortable) ways of working.

▨ Reduce the duration of the time spent in lower levels of the Y-Curve.

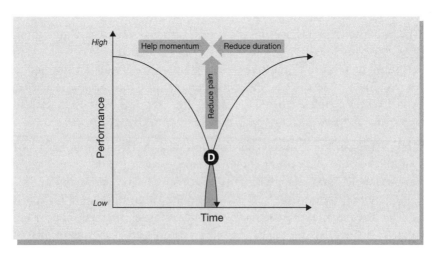

Figure 9.8 Coach's contribution

The shallow Y-Curve

This model works on the assumption that some degree of pain or resistance will occur and hence the coach's role is to help the client through this stage. However, it may well be the client has set clear goals, starts the journey and does not have any resistance or pain of change whatsoever. If this is the case then the Y-Curve will be so shallow as to be imperceptible, as in Figure 9.9. This is clearly a dream job for the coach as they can sit back and watch the client make the normally difficult transition from theory to action.

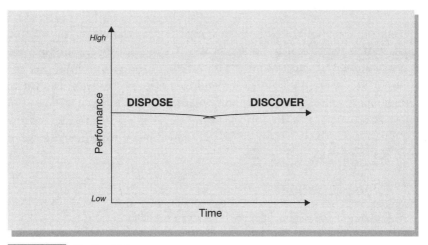

Figure 9.9   Shallow Y-Curve

However, (a) I don't believe that this happens very often, and (b) it might just be that the client is faking it. No matter what the change process and the displayed passion the client has for making the change, I tend to work on the basis that there will always be some small part of the change journey that the client will have a problem with, and if this small problem is not dealt with promptly it can grow and eventually cause the whole process to stall or collapse:

■ The potential marathon runner who struggles to get out of bed on a Sunday morning after a night out with the mates.

■ The person who has gone back to college in a bid to go for promotion but has an anxiety attack before a major exam.

■ The runner who wins all their races, but then finds they are racing against their nemesis – that one person they have never been able to beat (and whom they believe they are incapable of beating).

For example, starting WizOz was and is one of the most significant changes in my life. However, there have been times when fear, anxiety, despair and outright laziness have set in and I went scurrying to the papers to look for a 'proper' job. I am lucky that when the dips occur I have people who will help me through the Y-Curve. Sometimes these colleagues simply let me dump my fears and concerns and once the shadows are surfaced I am happy to move on. Other times they give me a kick up the backside and help me to get back into the groove. The coach must be constantly attuned to the client's mental, emotional and physical state and be prepared to spot if and when the client enters the doldrums and dissent area and then take the appropriate action.

It is this that presents us with the next aspect of the change stage – defining just what is the role of the coach at the D-Spot. Is their role to push the person through it and force them to dispose of the past and discover the future? Is it to simply hold their hand in a step-by-step way? Or is it to simply be there for them to support whatever decision they make (even if the coach believes it is the wrong one or one taken out of short-term panic or fear)? This is the issue considered in the next part of the Change stage in the 7Cs framework.

Coaching questions

Mobilization – ready to go	▨ What is your next action?
	▨ Can you describe what you will do and when you will do it?
	▨ Do you need any resources to make this happen?
	▨ What shall I do if you go into the doldrums?
Resistance – is there any?	▨ What might prevent you from doing this?
	▨ Do you have any fears about taking the steps?
	▨ When you think about doing it, what goes through your mind?
	▨ What are you thinking about the next step? What do you feel?
	▨ How should I react if you get angry about the pain of change?
	▨ How do you typically behave when resisting things?
Dispose – able to let go	▨ What do you like most about the old ways?
	▨ Are you prepared to give it up? Why?
	▨ Is there anything you don't really want to give up or let go of?
	▨ How long will it take to let go?
	▨ What do you want me to do if you don't let go?

Discover – looking forward	■	What are you looking forward to?

Discover – looking forward

- ■ What are you looking forward to?
- ■ Is there anything you need to learn to move forward?
- ■ Is there anything you might find difficult to learn?
- ■ How long will it take to acquire the new skills?
- ■ What can I do to help you learn the new way of working?
- ■ What have you learned recently? Do you have a preferred style of learning?

Change – make it happen

Speech is conveniently located midway between thought and action, where it often substitutes for both.

John Andrew Holmes

The coach can only ever help something to happen. The day they make the client take action they have moved from the role of coach to that of performance manager. The consequence is that they then own the issue and the client becomes subordinate to and dependent on the coach. But what can the coach do when the client repeatedly says that they will get up for the early morning jog but remains in bed; the aspiring manager repeatedly fails to attend management briefings; or the person who wants to reduce the long hours they work keeps stopping late in the office? Does the coach have to step in and take a more commanding or directive stance or is it best to let the client live through this stage and come to his or her own conclusions about why change is not being mobilized.

One of the ways to address this is to presume that the client will find this stage difficult and prepare a clear strategy in advance to deal with inactivity – to establish prior to entering the Change stage, when push comes to shove, which rules will govern the choices the coach has to make to help the client progress. In deciding this, the coach will need to agree what underlying ethos will drive the mobilization. Will it be one where the client owns the mobilization process and decides their personal rate of mobilization? Or will the coach own the process and be responsible for making it happen, as seen in Figure 9.10.

❝ The coach will need to agree what underlying ethos will drive the mobilization. ❞

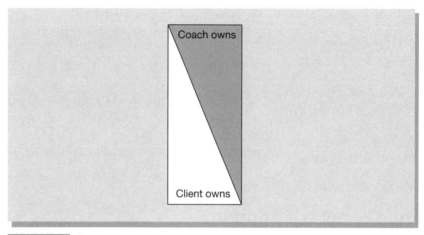

Figure 9.10   Change spectrum

Although there are degrees between the two extremes, any change will often have a bias in one direction. At one end of the spectrum the client takes all the responsibility for making it happen and the coach is there to provide empathic support. At the other end of the spectrum, the coach has the right to drive and trigger behavioural action and is allowed to get the client out of bed to ensure they go for the morning run.

When the client owns the mobilization process the upside is that they accept responsibility, can track their learning and are not dependent on the coach. However, the downside is that they may just never do it, or the mobilization can take for ever.

When the coach is in the driving seat the upside is that it happens, there is clear direction and the client is in no doubt as to what has to be done and by when. The downside is that dependency is created and the coach can set themselves up for the blame game if it goes wrong downstream. This is because at this level of command, although behaviours will have been modified, the client may feel they are taking the action under duress.

The net result is that when a client asks about the difficulty and length of time associated with the Change stage they might need to be educated about the trade-offs to be made. For example, a client who wants to improve their golf handicap has a decision to make. Do they look for a quick implementation, on the premise that it will happen but they will be heavily dependent on the coach? Or do they take a longer view and ask the coach to help them to discover a natural style? Although the coach can help facilitate the decision, the ultimate responsibility for the judgement must be down to the client.

Change levels

One way to help the client make sense of the change process is to offer a simple tool that can describe the levels of mobilization that sit across the change spectrum, where at one end the coach takes charge of the process and at the other the coach simply supports the client while they make all the choices. Working from one end to the other it is possible to identify six types of change:

▓ **Command:** Coach owns the change and does not delegate ownership of the mobilization to the client.

▓ **Helm:** Coach gives away some level of control and does not have absolute power over the direction of the project but still retains significant authority over the direction of the change process.

▓ **Agree and negotiate:** The coach gives away significant areas of the power. But they do this through agreement because of the desire to ensure that the mobilization does not stall.

▓ **Nudge:** The coach has conceded over 50 per cent of the power to effect change to the client. What they do though is keep a presence and encourage the client to take small steps to make the change happen.

▓ **Guide:** The coach's role is to now help the client understand more about the change. This is primarily an educational intervention where the role of the coach is almost that of teacher.

▓ **Empathy:** The coach shows understanding of the potential problem and offers the client time and space to acclimatize to their change.

At any time in the change process the coach has to make a choice as to the most appropriate level of intervention to help the client deliver their outcomes. Much of this choice will be based on the coach's prior experience with the client, the client's level of comfort about taking ownership of the mobilization and the speed that both wish to progress at.

Figure 9.11 outlines the process of managing a client through the various levels. Consider someone who asks the coach to help them prepare for running a marathon. They have done some general running before, but this would be a really big step for them. At the opening conversation the client admits that although they are keen to run the marathon, they do struggle with self-motivation and on previous occasions when they have tried to prepare they have failed to sustain the activity.

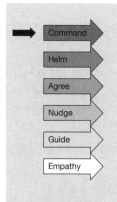

At this stage of the contract the coach will take quite a commanding role and ensure that the client actually does the necessary work. The coach books a series of training sessions, calls the client before the session and works with them at the training ground. This way the coach can ensure that the mobilization takes place and there is no chance for the change process to stall at the first gate.

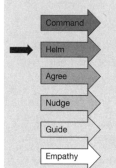

The coach works with the client in a directive way but gives them options. They agree the activities that need to take place each week but will leave the timing and scheduling of the session up to the client. They might not attend all of the sessions but will not tell the client which sessions they will attend, so the sense of control is still present.

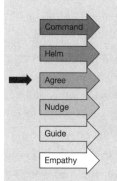

A few weeks into the schedule and the client appears to be self-managing their training programme. At this stage the coach sets up an agreement with the client. The coach will work with them to agree a training schedule but will only attend the weekend sessions. In return the client will call the coach after each session to give them an update on progress.

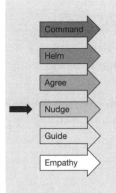

At this stage the client has proved they are able to self-manage the training schedule and do not need an overly directive style. However, both coach and client recognize that slippage can occur, so they agree that an occasional prompt is appropriate. This might be occasional spot checks or progress checks. The nudges might also be prompted where the coach spots that the client is slipping.

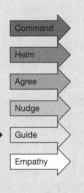

Both client and coach are now confident about the ability to self-maintain the change process, so the coach's role becomes a very low-intervention model. This consists of occasional feedback on observation of the client's action and suggestion on areas where techniques might be improved. The coach may either offer guidance on the technique changes or source experts who are able to guide the client in certain areas.

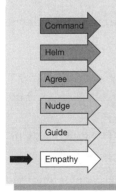

At this stage the client has the motivation and knowledge to make the change. The coach decides to back off and basically 'be there' for the client as and when problems arrive. At this point they are not making any primary interventions and control is wholly with the client. The consequence is that the client owns the process, is not dependent on the coach and has effectively moved to a position where they are self-coaching.

Figure 9.11   Managing a client through the various stages

Underpinning this process are a number of key points:

▪ The point of entry on to the different change levels will be dependent upon the client's needs and experience. There is no right point of entry, only what works for the client and helps with the mobilization process.

▪ The direction of intervention can be in two ways. The coach may start at the command point and move down to the empathic levels through a number of stages. Alternatively they might begin at the empathic end and have to move up to the command level because the client is struggling to get mobilized.

▪ Where the client is experienced in personal change they may open at the empathic level and stay there all the way through the mobilization stage.

▪ The switch between the levels can be rapid and in many cases instantaneous. At one point the coach may have to adopt a command approach (i.e. getting them out of bed) but once on the running machine can drop back to the empathic as the client has woken up to their failure and taken control again.

The important thing to note is that there is no right option with the CHANGE tool. The coach and client need to agree the following:

▪ The degree of latitude the coach has to regulate control over the client.

▪ The type of intervention the client prefers or expects.

▪ What preference you (as the coach) have (often coaches will favour one particular type of intervention based upon their psychological preference and personal beliefs).

▪ What budget is available to support the intervention since the cost of delivering each of the levels will vary quite considerably, both for short and long-run costs.

▪ What support processes are available since these will vary according to the type of change effected.

However, in most cases there are no miracle cures or single-shot solutions to mobilize change. The delivery of sustainable value through change involves introducing and sustaining multiple policies, practices and procedures across a range of levels on the change model.

Coaching questions

Command   ■ Can you let me know when the action is completed?

Helm   ■ You can take one of three possible steps – which would you prefer?

Agree   ■ If I do . . . , will you . . . ?
            ■ If you can do this then I will be able to . . .

Nudge   ■ Have you thought about . . .
            ■ Why don't you try to . . .

Guide   ■ This is how it works . . .
            ■ Have you tried talking with . . . to get their ideas?

Empathy   ■ How do you feel about this change?
            ■ What will you do next?
            ■ Is there anything that concerns you about moving forward?

John's journey

At this point John and Julie had fully understood the current situation, had considered various actions that could be undertaken and had decided on the first one to consider. This was to develop a basic network of potential peers prior to departure.

However, although John was keen to build a robust network, he kept finding reasons not to take the first step. Every time they agreed steps that he might take he would find reasons not to take the

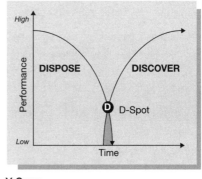

Y-Curve

action. The reasons seemed entirely valid and plausible, but after a time it became apparent that John was using delaying tactics to avoid taking action.

Julie raised this with John and in showing him the Y-Curve model made him realize that he had hit the doldrums. After working through it Julie helped John solve that part of the problem – he was finding it difficult to let go of the notion that networking was a cynical ploy used by sales agents to sell timeshares. He had a mental map of networking as a duplicitous model that made him feel really uncomfortable.

Julie helped him to address this by setting some homework where John would undertake some research on the principles of networking. He would read a number of books on networking that used an alternate approach. Julie also agreed to put him in touch with some of her colleagues who used networking as a social tool rather than a selling tool. This allowed John to let go of his preconceptions and then move into the discovery phase where he began to learn how to make contact with potential colleagues.

In helping to mobilize action Julie had made a conscious decision to intervene on a particular level of the CHANGE model. She knew that John needed to overcome a block and that any further delay might see him give up altogether. So for this reason she felt that the empathic level was not appropriate. Although she could have gone in at a more prescriptive level, because John had been making such good headway she was loath to risk any chance of building a new dependency.

CHANGE levels

For this reason the guide level seemed most appropriate. The two forms of education were from the desk research that he would carry out and a softer form of instruction, namely through conversation.

Had these interventions failed to mobilize then Julie might have considered moving up the CHANGE levels into the harder form of mobilization. But this would have brought with it certain consequences that she would have discussed with John.

10

Confirm – measure the change

The story so far

So far commitment has been established and both sides are comfortable in their relationship. The coach understands both the person and the picture they have painted and this picture has been tested to ensure that the client is operating at fact rather than fantasy level. The primary solutions have been developed, tested and put into place.

Enter the Confirm stage

The Confirm stage is the point where the pain really kicks in. It is the need to stand on the scales (full of dread) after the night out at the restaurant; the end-of-year appraisal when all your terrible deeds and misdemeanours are paraded in the annual report; the athletic race where you finally get to see whether the investment in time and energy over the past three months will help deliver a place in the first three. No matter how we try to dress it up, in most cases people are afraid of the Confirm stage because it is the point where you have to look in the mirror and finally see the reality of a situation. Mike Moir, a colleague, once clarified this for me when he said that many change and coaching processes tend to follow a common pattern of Client, Clarify, Create and Change and then RUN . . . (Figure 10.1).

The RUN behaviour is where people find any option they possibly can not to have to face up to the reality of the situation. For example, people keeping one foot on the ground when on the scales, not opening the mail in the morning when in serious debt for fear of the next bill, or cancelling the next sales meeting rather than face up to the bad news that revenue is

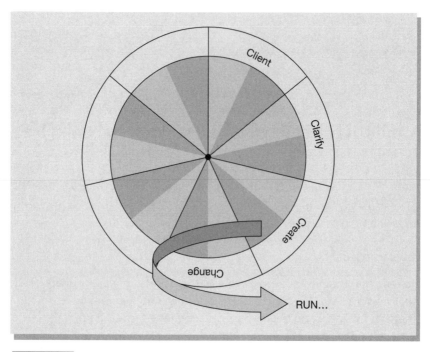

Figure 10.1 Run . . .

down. It is the run behaviour that is considered in this section and what the coach must do to help the client move from a need to hide, fake or ignore the measures and instead face up to the facts and where possible relish this stage as a chance to learn and move forward.

The two aspects considered in the Collaborative Coaching toolkit are:

- **Cockpit confirmation:** How the coach can help the client build a series of intrinsic reference points that determine when they are going off course and slippage is occurring.

- **Game playing:** People tend to play games when asked to measure their performance. By understanding the games the coach can both challenge the client to ensure they don't occur and teach the client to recognize when they are being played and hopefully take corrective action.

Cockpit confirmation

Man is the measure of all things.

Protagoras

One way that this stage of the coaching framework differs from the other areas is that it is designed to be undertaken when the client is on their own. Whereas many of the other tools are to be used in partnership with the client, with this one the goal is for the coach to help teach the client to use it when they are on their own.

Think about the flying instructor. A key part of their role is to help the trainee pilot fly the plane, but it is also to have the capability and process to determine when things are going wrong and take the necessary corrective action. In many sports the coach is not allowed onto the pitch or sporting field and so the client cannot use data from them to measure their performance. They must learn to self-monitor and again modify what they are feeling, thinking or doing so as to get back on track. Finally, probably the greatest coaching role in the world is that of the parent. The primary goal of any parent is to prepare the child to fly free from the family nest and be self-sufficient. With all of these aspects the key intervention is helping the person to self-assess or measure themselves rather than being the instrument that does the measurement. We can look at this in terms of the systems and processes that pilots use to land aircraft safely (Figure 10.2).

> ❝ **The primary goal of any parent is to prepare the child to fly free from the family nest and be self-sufficient.** ❞

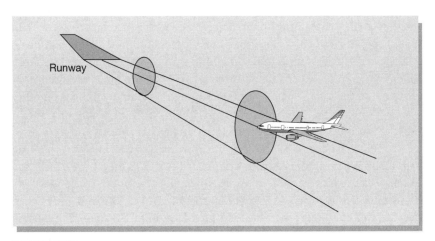

Runway

Figure 10.2 (ALS) Airline Landing System

Aeroplanes now land at airports that don't have hectares of vacant ground around them. They have to land in highly congested areas, where any deviation from the landing plan would result in disastrous consequences. To do this airlines use the "instrument landing system" (ILS) approach. Using this system (especially in conditions of poor visibility), an aeroplane fitted with appropriate equipment can approach an airport and receive high-precision signals from an instrument landing system. It is automatically guided down onto the runway, has its engines throttled back and its brakes applied, all without the aid of the pilot.

In the cockpit, the pilot has a flight display which indicates where the plane is in relation to the ILS beam. The pilot can use this display to define where they are in the descent, and whether they are off track and then make a corresponding adjustment to the landing. It is the ability to fly against a reference beam that enables the pilot to land in conditions that would otherwise make the flight impractical and dangerous. In the same way, an effective coach will help the client plot a directional heading and set a course to deliver their outcome.

In the same way that the ILS system will use flight data to determine whether a plane is off course, in a coaching partnership the coach should help the client define a set of bearings to indicate whether they are on or off course. For example, as a new motorbike rider, every time I go out on the bike I am still learning to understand and monitor what can be an alien set of sensory measures. I have to learn how to monitor my performance on the bike and take the necessary action if I seem to be riding in a way that could be dangerous.

After a few weeks of riding I began to learn how to tune into these sensory processes, such that I now know by the time I get to the bottom of the road whether I am ready to ride. In most cases it is fine, but I have started to watch for the telltale signs that something is not right. This might be a sense of emotional unease because of the weather or feeling tense because I have gone out in the middle of an argument; it might be that my mind is on other things (for example, trying to hit the deadline with this book); or it might be that I am not coordinated in using the throttle and brakes and so slide on the corner. Whatever it is, I have now learned to recognize when something internally is not right. When this happens I will stop for a while, push the internal pause button to slow things down and try to rectify the problem. Only once this is sorted do I go out on the bike. If I can't sort it then I have learned that it is best to go back for a cup of tea and then go out later. These signals act as my guidance system, giving me advance warning when something isn't right. The trick is to learn how to tune in to these subsystems, especially when you are not used to using such a deep intrinsic measurement system.

As discussed already, all human beings have three core dimensions that impact how they manage and respond to change. The key dimensions are affective (how people feel about the change), cognitive (what they know or understand) and behavioural (what they actually do). In confirming action around these three dimensions the key factors are as follows:

■ **Heart:** Evaluates the affective domain, which addresses the manner in which we deal with things emotionally, such as feelings, values, appreciation, enthusiasms, motivations and attitudes. Consider an athlete who is about to enter an important tournament. The heart factors to be measured might include how they feel about the tournament and the people in it and whether they are happy or irritated about the way it has been organized. One important tool to use at this stage is the e-Map outlined in the Client section of the book (Figure 10.3). By using this it can help the client to rapidly understand and measure their emotional state. Once understood they can then think about how to move to a more productive emotional domain.

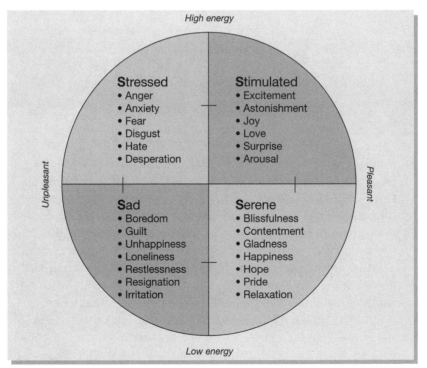

Figure 10.3 e-Map as a measurement tool

■ **Head:** Evaluates the cognitive domain, which includes the recall or recognition of specific facts, procedural patterns, and concepts that serve in the development of intellectual abilities and skills. Measurement of this dimension will be through helping the client to understand what they are saying to themselves. Are they using positive reinforcing statements such as 'I can win this race', 'I will get off the start line first', or do they use autopilot thoughts such as 'It is too difficult' or 'things will go wrong soon'? By setting a reference point of what language they should be using it helps them to measure deviation from this and so take the necessary corrective action (Figure 10.4).

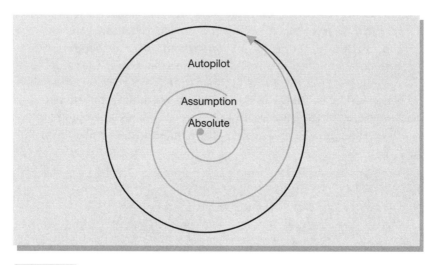

Figure 10.4   Head map

■ **Hand:** Measurement of this is by self-evaluating what is happening physically or behaviourally (Figure 10.5). This might be measured in terms of speed, precision or techniques in execution. The athlete preparing for a big race might notice that when they stretch they are feeling tension or physical stress in unusual areas, or they might notice a lack of rhythm when jogging around the track. This may give them a clue that the physical system is out of line and corrective action is needed before they start the race. Part of this is to recognize when bad habits might slip back in to the client's behaviour without them realizing it. Although I have broken the physical addiction to drink, I still notice how when I'm buying beer for others and some of it drips onto my hand, a dormant habit kicks in, i.e. to lick it off. I need to beware of the deep habits that can kick into place so easily, as considered in the Hand stage of the 3D model. Although my heart and head don't want to drink, it is hard to dispose of 25 years of physical conditioning.

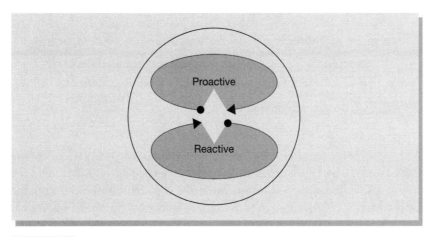

Figure 10.5   Hand map

We all use these intrinsic measures instinctively, the problem is that much of it takes place subconsciously. Because of this lack of overt and conscious awareness, reversion can happen because people don't pay attention to the affective, cognitive and behavioural signals that are being received. So the runner might view a sense of anxiety as pre-race upset and push it to one side. However, this anxiety can soon turn into stress and then into anger at the way other racers seem to be jostling them on the corners. It is the drift that causes so many problems in the coaching arena. Coaching people to make the initial change is relatively easy. When my son wanted to stop smoking I just offered to pay for his next holiday. This did the trick as it gave him the short-term inducement to stop. But I know that this isn't the real problem. The difficult bit will come when he next gets stressed and slowly slips to a point where his addicted hand suggests to the heart that one cigarette will not cause a problem and these two conspire against the logical head and win the day. Unless he is able to tune in to the minor relapses, he will find it difficult to prevent a major slippage.

> **❝ Reversion can happen because people don't pay attention to the affective, cognitive and behavioural signals. ❞**

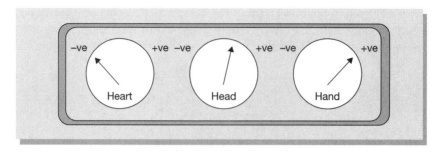

Figure 10.6 Cockpit confirmation

This is where the idea of the cockpit confirmation comes in, as seen in Figure 10.6. The coach's role is to take the topic being coached and then help the client define two outer parameters: what the client will be feeling, thinking and doing when the change is going well and what they will be feeling, thinking and doing when it is not going so well. As an example, consider Table 10.1. This sets out the cockpit measures that might be used to help a runner understand how to self-confirm while running the race.

Table 10.1 Cockpit measures

	Not going well (–ve)	*Going well (+ve)*
Heart	▓ Despair – why am I doing this? ▓ Anger – I knew I should have given this a miss.	▓ Excitement – at how great everything is. ▓ Anticipation – I could do this all day. ▓ Power – why can't everyone else keep up with me today?
Head	▓ Why am I here? ▓ Let's just get this session over with. ▓ This hurts. ▓ Something's wrong today.	▓ This is going well today. ▓ The way the training is going I'm feeling really good about the next race. ▓ Legs feel good today.
Hand	▓ Treading treacle. ▓ Shortened stride length. ▓ Upper body tight. ▓ Shoulders hunched. ▓ Breathing difficult.	▓ No stiffness. ▓ Balanced stride. ▓ Pushing off the toes. ▓ Upper body relaxed. ▓ Breathing easy.

Once the coach has helped the client to define the two outer parameters, the measures can be tracked for the duration of the engagement and beyond, to a point where the coach and client are satisfied that the value is locked in and will be sustainable once the engagement is closed. Hence, the three dimensions are tracked on a longitudinal basis, as seen in Figure 10.7.

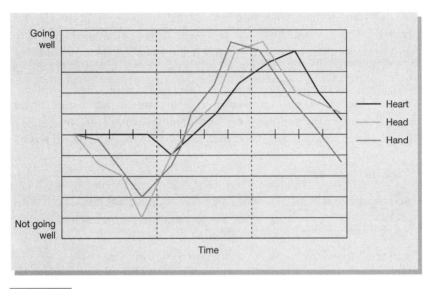

Figure 10.7   3-dimension tracking

At the very outset of the coaching relationship, the client and coach should agree what three dimensions should be measured both during the change and once complete. For the heart dimension try to agree what factors will be apparent if negative emotions are surfacing or if there are shadow factors causing anger or frustration. Also consider what signs will be apparent if things are going well, how to measure when the client is enthused and what techniques can be used to measure these dimensions. On a head level try to define what thoughts the client will have if things are not working and what mental maps they will need to have for the programme to be effective. Finally, from a hand perspective, if problems are surfacing what will people be saying and doing and conversely what will their behaviours and conversations be when things are going well? By defining dimensional criteria, it becomes easier to fly a precision approach and land the client's project on the spot every time.

For example, consider the coach working with a manager who desperately wants to improve their performance at work. Once the coach and client have defined the performance to be improved, they will want to install a measurement process that the client can use independently of the coach. If the manager wants to be a better interviewer, the Confirm model will be built around this. So the coach and client will first look at the great interview session that has been carried out and map how the client felt: what they were saying to themselves and what physical or behavioural patterns were evident. Once understood, the coach will help the client to think through a recent interview process that they were not happy with. The client will then indicate what they felt at the time, the types of things they were saying to themselves and what physical and behavioural routines were being played out. This will give them upper and lower boundaries against which the client can begin to measure. In this way the client can learn to continually self-monitor the three dimensions and recognize if things are beginning to falter and then take the necessary remedial action.

Coaching questions

Heart negative questions	▨ When things are not going well how do you feel?
	▨ What feelings can you recall the last time it didn't work so well?
Heart positive questions	▨ When things are great what are you feeling?
	▨ Can you describe what you felt the last time it went well?
Head negative questions	▨ When things are not going well what will you say to yourself?
	▨ When things are not going well what might you say to others?
Head positive questions	▨ When things are going well what will you say to yourself?
	▨ When things are going well what might you say to others?
Hand negative questions	▨ When things are not going well how will you behave?
	▨ When things are not going well what habits emerge?
Hand positive questions	▨ When things are going well what how will you behave?
	▨ When things are going well how might others describe your behaviour?

F-games

The best measure of a man's honesty isn't his income tax return. It's the zero adjust on his bathroom scale.

Arthur C. Clarke

Open any newspaper and the chances are that you will find stories that highlight the problem with the measurement stage. The measurement scams will fall into a number of camps, including:

■ Where people create measures that they know are attainable and hence offer a guaranteed outcome. These are not measures, just confirmation that the original target was correct, so the measurement process is a fake.

■ Where people put measures in place but don't really mean to use them because they have a solution or fix in mind and are convinced that they don't need measures to tell them what they already know.

■ Where complex measures are built, but at a shadow level so that when people know that they will not be achieved, they conveniently forget to undertake the measurement.

The idea in this section is to explore the common games that get played around the Confirm stage and then understand how to help the client avoid falling into such a trap.

The measurement process

Before we consider the games played in this area, it is useful to understand just what a typical measurement system or process might look like. In most cases the measurement processes are relatively consistent. Performance measurement helps to demonstrate that the person is moving in the right direction and is achieving the desired outcomes. They also help to identify the changes that need to occur in order to rectify any problems to achieve desired future goals.

Implementing measures

The coach must help the client to understand that their personal measurement system needs to be considered as a core process in its own right. Many coaches and clients fail to recognize this and take on a very laissez-faire approach to the Confirm stage. Only later are they surprised when the change doesn't stick and value is not added for the client. Besides all the emotional and logical problems with implementing a personal measurement system, the difficulty of collecting the data, putting it in the right format and presenting it in a way that makes sense to the coach and client takes more time and effort than most people are prepared to allow. Hence this is why the Confirm issue is set out as a separate stage in the coaching framework. It needs careful planning and the allocation of time and resources. Both coach and client need to be persistent and allocate regular meetings to monitor progress, as when things get sticky both players might start to wish that this stage would drop out of sight.

> **❝ Both coach and client need to be persistent and allocate regular meetings to monitor progress. ❞**

The ideal use of measures occurs when the client is able to act on the measures themselves without prompting or supervision. As already mentioned, the Confirm stage is not about reporting progress to the coach and waiting for further orders. The idea is that measures are to be used by the client rather than being used as pacifiers for the coach.

The steps seen in Figure 10.8 will all tend to be considered in some way or form in most measurement systems:

1 **Agree scope:** Identify the area or activity that needs to be measured.

2 **Define measures:** Establish the performance goal(s) or standards that will indicate whether the desired outcome is being achieved.

3 **Build system:** Develop the process by which the data will be gathered and analyzed. This will include who will manage the measurement process and when measurements will take place.

4 **Measure:** Collect data – observe any early trends and identify any corrective action that might need to be taken. Compare actual performance to defined goal(s).

5 **Take action:** Depending on the variation between measurements and goals, some form of corrective action may be required.

6 **Review outcome:** Confirm that both the measurement system and the desired outcome have been deployed with success.

However simple a process this might appear, it is one that is rarely used with any great enthusiasm or discipline. This is because the measurement stage is the place where people either play games or seek to ignore for fear of embarrassment. As a consequence there are three common sub-processes that can be seen in the Confirm stage.

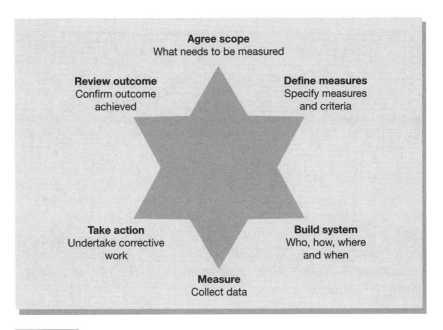

Figure 10.8   Star measurement process

Fake it

There is an old adage that what gets measured gets managed. In my experience this is often a fallacy. In many cases the adage might be what gets measured gets bluffed. This is the stage when the pigeons come home to roost and the pain of change really starts to hit home.

The faking it pattern can be seen in Figure 10.9. When considered in a coaching context this might be likened to the team manager who sets out the new performance measures they want to achieve (increase calls handled); they measure this using a simple sampling process each week and then look back to review the outcome and see how successful they have been. The problem is that by missing certain elements what has been omitted is the fact that this does not achieve the overall goal. The fact is that they are losing business because the attitude of the call reception team sucks. They are fed up and this shows in the way they speak to customers. They need to do some serious work around their motivation and call-handling process, but the absence of a tight scope nullifies any benefit from the process.

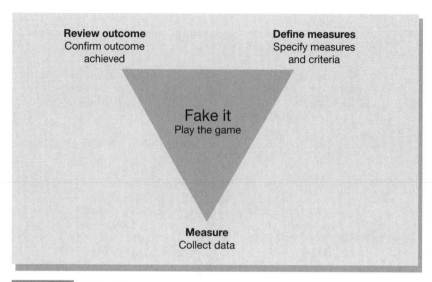

Figure 10.9 Faking it

When this happens a number of the core stages in the measurement cycle are conveniently forgotten or overlooked. The missing stages are:

- Agree scope.
- Build system.
- Take action.

In many cases people omit the first point (agree scope) because it means that they can conveniently ignore the final point (take action). If they meet the arbitrary measures, it allows them to feel good without getting any pain from the measurement process.

When faced with this the coach must begin to challenge the client's confirmation process. They should seek to ensure that the measurement process fits with a purpose within the overall coaching goal; that it deploys a system that gets real and valid data and not just data that can be used to meet the client's faking it needs; and that it is linked to hard, tangible action.

A word of warning with this one – we cannot assume that it is just the client who will use the faking it approach. Coaches are human and have egos. Some them are also self-employed or work in large organizations where results are necessary to pay the mortgage or further their career. It can be in the coach's interest to use a faking approach, possibly in collusion with the client or just through tacit and unspoken assumptions that it would be good for both to be perceived as delivering the agreed outcome. This is why it is so important to surface and talk about the Confirm stage at the start of the engagement, and thus before the emotional political forces step in that push people to make bad choices about how measurement is undertaken. If the process can be locked in at the start and both understand the reason why this full approach must be carried out, there is more chance that mutual collusion and deception will not occur.

This is important because the faking it model is and always will be a short-term, transitory solution. I can only stand on the scales with one foot on the floor for so long. At some point someone will mention that I seem to have put on weight or I need to upgrade my clothes by a size as the old ones 'seem to have shrunk'. The truth will always come out. All the faking it pattern does is to defer the day when reality finally bites.

Fix it

This pattern is also common and examples can be found when people are trying to become more effective by improving their time management. They might attend the latest course; spend a fortune buying the books, wall charts, expensive inserts and maybe even the software for their computer. The scope is agreed, system built and that is it, they are off busily writing goals, setting out clear sub-tasks and reviewing all of this on a daily basis. However, one day they are too busy to do the review so they put it off until tomorrow. A few days later the same happens so they decide it would be better to do the review on a weekly basis. This then shifts to a monthly basis and slowly fades away into nothingness as they revert to their old habits. But because they have not actually measured their improved performance by using the system they don't have to face the facts. This happens because people are so convinced that this is the right answer that they don't need to measure whether a real and sustainable gain has been achieved.

With this pattern (Figure 10.10) only the following steps are included:

- ■ Agree scope.
- ■ Build system.
- ■ Take action.

And the following are omitted:

- ■ Define measures.
- ■ Measure.
- ■ Review outcome.

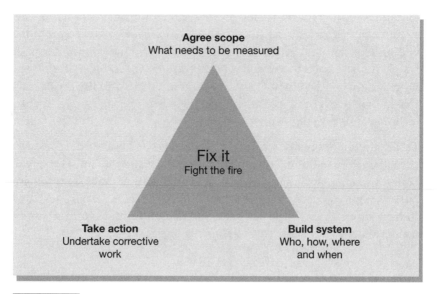

Figure 10.10 Fix it pattern

The steps included are all very activity based but with no need to take a reflective stance. They can be undertaken without any pain of looking in the mirror, whereas those omitted require the client to be quite specific about how they will measure success: to actually take time out to measure the outcome and then look at the data with some honesty and draw conclusions about their ability (or inability) to deliver sustainable value. Cleary, this is why the fix it pattern finds such favour, because it is painless but very action based.

> **This is why the fix it pattern finds such favour, because it is painless but very action based.**

Forgot it

As I look back over ten years of trying to beat the alcoholic addiction it is almost funny to see the measurement games that I played with others and myself. I played my share of faking it and fix it games and if I may say I played them extremely well. Another common game is the 'Oops, I forgot it was time to measure myself'. I would set amazing objectives, build systems and decide to do a review every Sunday morning to see how I had done with the cutting down. But the amazing thing was that come Sunday morning I always forgot. And the great thing about being a drunk was that I could blame the drink on the basis that I had a hangover.

We see this in other areas as well. The couple going through marriage guidance who conveniently forget to do their regular open reviews with each other, or the senior manager who forgets to follow the system of checking the corporate scorecard results each week. The great thing about forgetting is that we can all use the all-encompassing reason for failure to measure, which is 'I am only human'. The trouble is that if you find something that is really important to that person (their car, health or work), the chances are that they don't forget the things that need measurement with these.

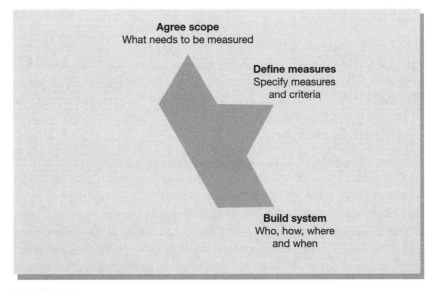

Agree scope
What needs to be measured

Define measures
Specify measures
and criteria

Build system
Who, how, where
and when

Figure 10.11 **Forgot it game**

The forgot it pattern can be seen in Figure 10.11. The key stages that have been covered include:

▦ Agree scope.

▦ Define measures.

▦ Build system.

And the three stages that have been conveniently forgotten are:

▦ Measure.

▦ Take action.

▦ Review outcome.

Now, you may have sensed from my tone in the introduction to this game that I don't believe in repeated forgetfulness. I do believe that people are human, but I also believe that people prioritize choices, and they prioritize against what is really important to them as opposed to what they say is important! So I spent all the money I saved on not drinking for four years and bought myself a Harley Davidson. Believe me, there is little chance that I will forget to measure the oil because I love this machine. But interestingly, I do regularly forget to check the oil on my clapped-out work vehicle – because it isn't that important to me. I might say it is and curse myself when the engine blows, but if I am honest with myself it is nowhere near as important as the bike.

And this is the crux of the matter – the level of importance. Beware the client who uses the 'I forgot' routine because in my experience it is a lie – not a blatant lie to you as the coach, but more worryingly a lie to themselves. Where this does occur the coach may well have to dig deep to surface why this happens and whether it is an indication of any deeper lack of interest in the coaching process.

Finally, although the Confirm stage by its very nature can tend to be quite factual and clinical, it is important to remember that there is a huge symbolic element associated with measurement. Just the fact that someone has turned up to the weekly weigh in, counted the money jar to see how much money they have saved on cigarettes that week, or simply asked the coach for feedback on performance can be a huge boost to their self-belief and confidence. In many cases the failure to measure can have more disastrous consequences than actually measuring and getting bad news. At least by measuring and getting feedback that all is not well the client has a chance to learn from the data. With no data there can be no learning.

Why Confirm?

It is all too easy for both the coach and client to not really pay sufficient attention to this stage. It is too easy to come up with simple measures that prove that the investment has been of value so that both players can celebrate their success and move on. It is far harder to have the courage and really ensure that the client does measure their outcomes and more importantly is left with a clear and robust measurement system that they can use once the engagement is complete. A failure to address this negates the whole purpose for the time investment of the coaching process. It will leave the client with a bitter taste in their mouth or a sense of guilt about not really having achieved the outcome. Finally, it slowly but relentlessly erodes the brand value of the coach. Brand is about repeat business. If your client doesn't shout about how great you are and you don't have measures to prove how great you are, then your brand will be pretty poor, if not non-existent.

Hence, even if the client does not want to focus on the Confirm stage, it is paramount that the coach does – otherwise you are left with little tangible evidence to prove that you have added value in the coaching contract. Where the client either knowingly or unknowingly suggests that confirmation is not important, you have a commercial and ethical responsibility to push them on to this stage. This is why it is important to test the client's readiness and willingness to measure at the outset, before the engagement starts. If you get indications that they will not measure, I suggest that you don't engage in a relationship with them.

Coaching questions

Agree scope	■ What is the outcome you want?
Define measures	■ How can it best be measured?
	■ How will you know good?
	■ What are the quantitive measures that can be used?
	■ What are the qualitative measures that can be used?
Build system	■ How will you gather the data?
	■ How will you analyze the data?
	■ Who will gather that data?
	■ When will the measurements take place?
Measure	■ How will you identify any trends?
	■ How will you compare actual performance to defined goal(s)?
Take action	■ How will you identify what corrective action may be required?
Review outcome	■ What process will you use to confirm that the measurement system has been a success?
	■ How will you know whether the outcome has been achieved?

John's journey

After a few weeks Julie wanted to help John develop a personal measurement system. The goal was to move the need for Julie to provide the impetus and processes to help John know how things were going and for him to automatically know how he was doing and when to take corrective action.

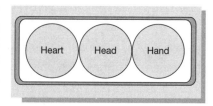

Cockpit confirmation

Julie introduced him to the cockpit mode and they used this to map John's feelings, thoughts and behaviours while trying to build the network. John found the process really useful, although he found the practical aspect of measuring his emotions a challenge. He was able to look back and describe how he had felt in previous situations, but found the process of measuring real-time affections difficult.

Julie decided that this would be an important process for John and they agreed to allocate some time helping him to become more proficient at emotional measurement. They did this by setting a series of repeat alarms on his personal organizer. Every hour during the day when the alarm sounded he would map where his feelings were against the e-Map. He would then review this data with Julie at the following meeting.

After a while John became really quite proficient at mapping and measuring his feelings, thoughts and behaviours and was able to use these as a way to take corrective action when he started to drift off course during the networking process.

Once John became proficient at the self-measuring process, Julie helped him to understand and think more about the process of measurement and the problems that could arise. She took him through the F-games model. They agreed that it would be all too easy for John to slip into a sanitized form of measurement where he focused more on keeping Julie happy and hiding from the truth. They agreed that part of the weekly session would be spent reviewing the Confirm process and ensuring that he was being rigorous in his self-measurement.

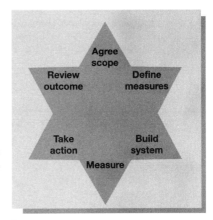

F-games

11

Continue – make sure it will last

The story so far

In the beginning commitment was tested and established, and with this a trust-based relationship was formed. The coach then spent time ensuring that they understood both the person and their desired picture. Once the picture was tested, robust solutions were identified and put into place. With the successful deployment of the solutions the client then learned how to self-regulate and take action when measures suggested that they were not on target.

Enter the Continue stage

This stage is about ensuring that all the work put in on the coaching journey yields value that will last and not just fade over time once the client reverts to their old ways of feeling, thinking and behaving. Hence, the concern is less about what happens within the coaching process but rather what happens after it has been closed.

If you consider Figure 11.1, in the initial stage the coach works with the client to help realize a personal change. Once the change is complete, the coach departs. Once the engagement is over, one of three things can happen: the client's performance might deteriorate, it might stay the same or, hopefully, it might continue to improve without the assistance of the coach. Both the coach and the client need to be aware that there are reinforcing and repressive forces acting upon the change and, for sustainability, they must ensure that any action plan includes an approach to managing these.

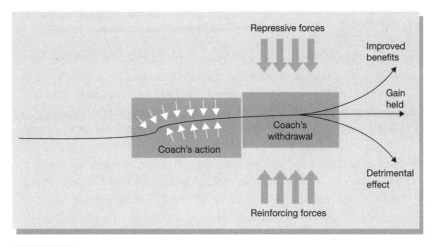

Figure 11.1 Sustainability curve

Hence the Continue stage is about making sure that the client will be self-sufficient and able to stand on their own two feet once the coaching session or journey is complete. However, just look at the list of words in Table 11.1. Why is it that so many clients see their coaching assignment in terms of words from the left-hand column while the end result might be described by words from the right-hand column?

Table 11.1 Anticipated vs actual outcomes

Intent	Long-term outcome
Action	Abort
Better	Bluff
Cure	Chaos
Deliver	Delay
Easy	Embarrassment
Faster	Fails

Although some of this may seem harsh, I am sure that you have been in situations either as a coach or client where sustainable change has been realized. But I do come across a lot of situations where this is not the case. And if we want to understand how to ensure that our clients achieve value through sustainable change, it is imperative to look more deeply at this issue and explore just why change doesn't last.

The six patterns described in the table above may be explored further and seen as the following:

- **Action/Abort:** Often clients are rushing into action like Custer at the charge, only to find out that they can go no further because they are out of resources. For example, in any war the unsung heroes tend to be troops who manage the supply channels. An army can rush ahead as fast as it wants, but eventually it will run out of food and fuel. At this point all the bravado and bravery will have little value without a few cans of fuel. This is the same in a coaching environment: people will charge from the gate only to find that three months later they have run out of time, energy and maybe cash. A friend of mine starting college was promised that they would pass – not because of their great intellectual prowess but simply because the drop-out rate in the first three months was huge, and in most cases those who stayed the course passed the course. The coach must never forget to ensure that the client does not fall into the trap of being over-enthusiastic and under-resourced.

- **Better/Bluff:** Things often get better before they get worse. Like the marathon runner who changes his trainers when he is under-performing, there might be a short-term improvement in performance but in reality, unless he resolves the fact that he needs to actually put in more hours each week, the issue has not been resolved. In this case the only person they are kidding is themselves and hence it is a foolish and wasteful bluff.

- **Cure/Chaos:** In this case the cure is worse than the original problem. A doctor may happily prescribe antidepressants for a depressed patient. But unless the doctor tries to understand the root cause of the depression, they are leading the individual down a rocky road to possible long-term addiction. An insidious cycle of shared dependency can be generated with this approach. This is the danger where clients look for causes to solve the problem, but unless the deeper issues are understood things are made worse.

- **Deliver/Delay:** As a coach you may help the client to make a change on the assumption that it has been effective. The problem is that you might not be around to see the impact of your actions. If you are not around in six months' time how do you know that you haven't just delayed the problem?

- **Easy/Embarrassment:** As a coach it is all too easy to use tried and tested techniques on the basis that what worked before will work again. You are like the man with a hammer who believes that all problems can be fixed with a nail. The danger is that after trying for the fifth time to push 'a square peg into a round hole', you might have to accept (with some embarrassment) that the easy, quick-fix solution might not be the most appropriate. Just because one client looks like another, it doesn't mean that solutions can be easily replicated.

❝ The easy, quick-fix solution might not be the most appropriate. ❞

■ **Faster/Fails:** The pressure valve on a cooking pot or the governor on a steam engine are examples of how things are set to operate at their optimum level. In the same way, any human system will have an optimum level at which it will operate and any effort to push this over the limit will be frustrating for the coach and damaging for the client. The coach must always beware that they are not trying to manage the process at a pace that suits them rather than the client.

As a coach you are being asked to help to deliver a sustainable change in the client's world. However, this world is one that you can never truly understand because it has deep and dark forces that will seemingly conspire to act against the desire to deliver a high-value change that will last. The six patterns listed above offer only a taste of the deep issues that affect the chance of getting a sustainable outcome. If you and the client are to stand any chance of delivering sustainable value then it pays to expend some real effort to understand some of the more subtle forces that can both help and disable change in one swoop.

To aid this process two tools are considered. The first is to understand what are the subtle forces that conspire to make change fail and what the client can do to compensate for these forces. The second is to try to help the client appreciate that there are relatively few quick fixes to a real coaching issue. In most cases they have to take quality time out to really look inside and appreciate how their sense of personal passion and purpose will impact the sustainability of any outcome.

Buckets and balloons

It's not that some people have willpower and some don't. It's that some people are ready to change and others are not.

James Gordon, M.D.

It is important for clients to understand that the desire to slip back into old habits is normal and to be expected. This does not mean that something is wrong or that the client doesn't really want to change.

Consider the person who wants to give up smoking. Even once they have stopped for a few weeks they will be surrounded by a multitude of stimuli or triggers that will seem to conspire to make them have just one drag for old times' sake. Common triggers include being around people who smoke, getting paid and having spare cash, drinking alcohol, social situations, and certain affective states, such as anxiety, depression or joy. Triggers for reversion are many and the coach's role is to help the client prepare for this and develop a clear and actionable place to address such situations.

To explain the ideas of triggers, coaches need to draw upon the ideas introduced in the Client stage of the model. In the same way that Pavlov's dog developed associations with the bell that triggered a desire to act, clients can learn to understand their triggers and manage the compulsion to respond. This stage is about mapping and managing the forces that trigger reversion and finding ways to counter the forces and so prolong the sustainability of the coaching outcome.

Identifying buckets

The triggers or cues that stimulate slippage can be viewed as 'buckets'. This term is used because it helps to describe the impact the triggers can have on someone who is seeking to make a change. Consider a client who has real problems with managing their time. They believe that only by dealing with this problem can they get the desired promotion, which in turn will lead to their ability to buy a new house. The problem is that every time they attend a time management course they leave the event full of grand dreams, real belief in themselves and wonderful processes, but a week later they have slipped into the same old bad habits.

We can track this personal journey into reversion by looking at what happens on day one after the course. Although they enter work with a personal action plan that outlines their key goals, primary tasks and regular actions for the day, the moment they get into work it turns out a colleague has gone sick. On top of that their boss has found a 'can you just' job for them to do, then just before lunch one of their problem customers raises a complaint about the service given the previous week (Figure 11.2). At this point each new trigger or cue feels like added weight that they have to carry round, and a load that seems to drag them back to the old behaviour of fire fighting and immediate responses, thus throwing the long-term plan out of the window.

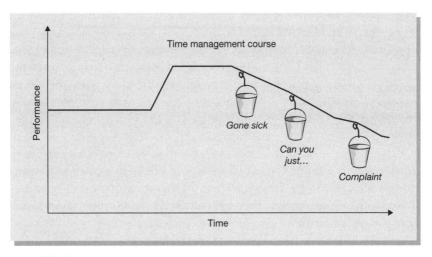

Coaches need to work with clients to develop a comprehensive list of their buckets. If the client becomes overwhelmed when asked to identify triggers, it can be helpful to concentrate on identifying the major buckets that have occurred in recent days or weeks. These might be things like association with certain people, being in particular offices, or hearing the wrong song. For me I soon realized that in trying to give up drink a huge bucket was being hungry. For some reason, when I was starving I had a real desire for a drink and also lost a lot of the willpower to say no. I had no idea why this happened, but the fact that I was able to identify it and take remedial action was enough. I could have spent masses of time investigating and contemplating why it happened but it was easier to recognize it and just avoid the potential bucket.

Blow up the balloons

Clearly the simplest way to avoid the bucket of being hungry was to ensure that I never got beyond being peckish. The moment I felt the real hunger pangs coming on I would ensure that I had some apples or a light snack (in reality it was probably a bag of chips). However, by finding a response mechanism to deal with the bucket I managed to lighten what was potentially a heavy load that could drag me down.

On the basis that buckets are triggers and cues that the client has to deal with, the coach's role is to help them prepare a strategy to respond and overcome the debilitating impact. In simple terms the coach's job is to help take away some of the weight of the buckets and lighten the load for the client. In an ideal world this might be possible, but in many cases once the load is there it can be difficult to erase. Another alternative is to lighten the load by attaching a balloon to it. So when the manager is offered the chance to present to the board, they don't want to be in the position where they have to say no and explain that they are nervous about public presentations. It is sometimes easier to go to acting classes and learn how to put on a show. The nervousness may still be there, but by learning certain acting techniques these can help manage some of the deep fears they have about talking in front of people. This minimizes the problem and saves any potential embarrassment.

❝ Another alternative is to lighten the load by attaching a balloon to it. ❞

In the case of someone who has been on the time management course and faces the barrage of buckets on the first day back at the office, they might develop a series of balloons to help them overcome the panic of a Monday in the office. This might be to block out the first hour for 'stuff', send an e-mail to their boss telling them about the course and the point made by the course tutor about managers who pass down last-minute jobs, and create a standard response template for customer complaints that allows them time to breathe and fit it into the daily schedule (Figure 11.3). None of this is rocket science, but the trick is not to return to work assuming that all will

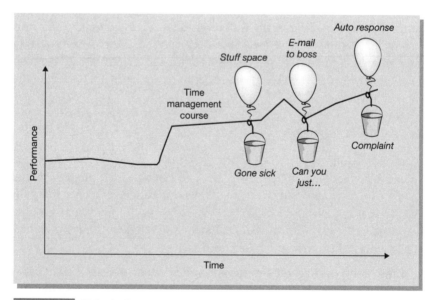

Figure 11.3   Using balloons to combat buckets

go right. The trick is to return to work and assume that things will go wrong. Assume that slippage and behavioural reversion occur (because they always have before) and develop appropriate response strategies.

Importantly, this is not about negative thinking and setting a route map in their head that will drive failure. It is about developing a level of personal honesty to say that I am human and if reversion has happened before then the chances are that it will happen again. By preparing for the worst it allows the coach and client to develop the appropriate strategies that can compensate for human frailty.

Intrinsic and extrinsic buckets and balloons

Once we understand the notion of buckets as forces that trigger reversion and balloons as factors that help overcome such forces, we can delve deeper inside these forces to understand what actually happens. In understanding the notion of triggers and cues that provoke a reversion to old feelings, thoughts and behaviours we are delving into the territory of stimulus-response theory.

The terms stimulus and response are quite fundamental to understanding the coaching model and in particular understanding how the client behaves in certain situations. If we get some dust up our nose, we sneeze: the dust is the stimulus; sneezing is the response. A dentist misses the tooth and sticks the prod in our gum and we scream: the prod is the stimulus; the scream and jerk are the response.

These are examples of reflexes. These are automatic, both natural and learned responses to external stimuli, over which we have little or no conscious control. The goal of the coach and client is to understand what extrinsic stimuli will act as a trigger and importantly what is happening intrinsically to create the bucket.

The key point here is that a bucket is virtually always intrinsic – the trigger is extrinsic – but it is our chosen response to a stimulus that creates the problem. For example, many food scientists have reported chocolate to be the single most craved food and some researchers suggest that chocolate is addictive. For some people the sight of a chocolate bar will create an urgent need to consume, whereas others can happily not touch chocolate for years. So the external trigger is the sight or smell of the chocolate. For someone on a diet and with a love of the sweet stuff this may turn into a bucket that seeks to drag them down to the pit of craving or addiction. For other people this smell has no impact and so is not a bucket.

This brings us again to that critical aspect about coaching – namely, choice. Where coaching works, people make the optimum choice and stick with it: coaching fails where people fail to control choice. It really is as simple as that.

Let's imagine the dieter again who has done well for a week or so. They walk into the kitchen and there on the table are two things – a bar of chocolate and a stick of celery. It is at that moment that all the preparing, coaching and pain that they have gone through to lose 5lb comes to a head. Do they pick up the stick of celery or the bar of chocolate? At this precise moment we have the choice point seen in Figure 11.4. Whether it is preparing for promotion, doing Open University coursework or getting up at 5am for an early-morning run – there is a micro point when a choice has to be made. This is the point at which all the work the coach has been doing comes to a head. This model is on the Continue stage of the framework because in most cases the choice point will occur when the coach is not around to offer the emotional, logical or physical support that might be needed to make the best choice.

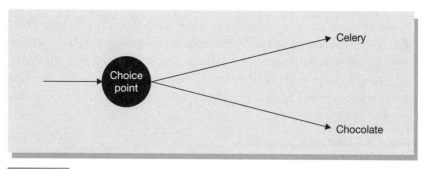

Figure 11.4   Choice point

The non-ethical and short-term coach will get the person operating effectively while they are around and then leave them to their own devices. The ethical and long-term coach will work on the principle that reversion does happen and their job is to prepare the client for the time when it begins to occur. They must help deconstruct explicitly what the triggers are that cause buckets to appear and then help develop balloons to compensate for the weight.

One way to explore this in more depth is to look at the buckets and balloons using the 3D model outlined in the Client stage of the framework, when thinking about the notion of triggers to break the response back against the three dimensions of Heart, Head and Hand (Figure 11.5).

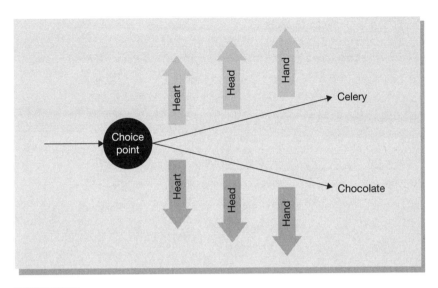

Figure 11.5   Triggers

For example, if we consider someone who has a fear of presenting to the management board, they might face a choice point – to present or find an excuse not to be involved. For the Heart it might trigger guilt when they think about the thought of facing these 'important people', it might trigger Head buckets as they start to convince themselves that they can go sick and no one will notice. Alternatively, the Hand dimension might kick in as they start to physically shake and perspire in reaction to being asked to present.

The coach should work with the client to identify all possible triggers that might cause a problem. As the triggers are mapped they discover what associated response the trigger will elicit to cause a potential bucket, as seen in Table 11.2. This might be blatantly obvious, such as when someone shouts at the client or criticizes their work they become anxious or defensive. Or it may be more subtle – for example, when someone walks into work and they smell the aromas associated with their particular workplace they might automatically become depressed.

> **❝ The coach should work with the client to identify all possible triggers that might cause a problem. ❞**

Table 11.2	Potential buckets

Potential heart buckets	Potential head buckets	Potential hand buckets
▨ Depression	▨ Symbolic association	▨ Conditioned responses
▨ Anxiety	▨ Established thought patterns	▨ Smell
▨ Boredom	▨ Self-criticism	▨ Touch
▨ Fear	▨ Low attention span	▨ Taste
▨ Anger	▨ Procrastination	▨ Tiredness
▨ Greed	▨ Negative thinking patterns	▨ Drugs and drink
▨ Guilt		▨ Pain
▨ Sadness		▨ Hunger
▨ Loneliness		

This can be a complex model because a number of things might happen. It may be that one extrinsic trigger will prompt one associated bucket – such as seeing a spider provokes fear and nothing else. It may be that seeing a picture of a spider provokes fear which leads to automatic recall of a time when they have been touched by a spider. Or it may be that seeing the spider provokes fear, which leads to negative thoughts that in turn trigger a physical action of running away. The important point is that different people will respond in different ways and that this response is in most cases a choice. The goal of the coach and client is to build a theoretical map of what will happen or actually set up a situation and watch how the client behaves under test conditions.

Avoiding triggers

Part of the continuance strategy is often to simply avoid or bypass the triggers before they even happen. So the alcoholic may walk a different route home to avoid passing the bar where their friends drink, or the manager may ensure that they don't come in contact with the director who causes them emotional problems. When coaching people who want to leave the life of organizational man or woman and set up on their own, one of my first challenges is for them to break many of the associations with other 'company' people and find new relationships with people who have a different mindset.

There are a variety of strategies that can be used to avoid triggers. These include the following:

■ **Distraction:** In many cases, an effective strategy for coping with conditioned triggers is distraction, especially doing something physical. This might include taking a walk, playing sport, going for a swim or learning to play the guitar. The content is pretty well immaterial as it is the distraction that is key. Maybe prepare a list of reliable off-putting activities that can be used when the desire to revert is triggered. Preparation of such a list in advance can help reduce the risk of reversion.

■ **Discussion:** When clients have supportive friends and colleagues, talking about the issue when it occurs is a very effective strategy and can help reduce the feelings of anxiety and vulnerability that often accompany it. It can also help because colleagues may offer their experiences of attempting to make similar behavioural changes.

■ **Recalling the bad times:** When experiencing a need to revert to old habits, many people have a tendency to remember only the positive effects of previous habits. They often forget the negative consequences. Thus, when experiencing a desire to revert, it is often effective for them to remind themselves of the benefits of not behaving that way and the downsides of the old behaviour. This way, clients can remind themselves that they really will not feel better if they go back to their old ways. Maybe get the client to list on a card the reasons they want to change and the negative consequences of use and to keep the card in their wallet or briefcase. If they look at the card when they are confronted by a desire to revert, it may remind them of the negative consequences of cocaine use at a time when they are likely to recall only the high spots.

■ **Using self-talk:** Often clients will experience a high level of self-talk that accompanies a desire to revert. This might be a phrase such as 'just this time', 'it is my birthday' or 'just a treat', all giving rise to permission to slip. The thing is that the inner dialogues are often so deeply established that clients are not aware of them. Autopilot thoughts associated with reversion often have a sense of urgency and exaggerated dire consequences (e.g. 'I have to use now,' 'I'll fail if I don't use,' or 'I can't do anything else until I use'). In coping with this, it is important both to help the client recognize the autopilot thoughts and to counter them effectively. To help patients recognize these thoughts coaches can point out cognitive distortions that occur. One way to do this is to slow down the tape – to take step by step what happened with the inner voice. Once mapped it can be easier to counter or confront the distorted logic being used in the conversations.

Prepare for failure

Finally, in some cases it can help to prepare in advance for a lapse: to say these things happen and don't let one slip cause a collapse in the whole process. So often diets fail because the person sneaks one chocolate bar. Once the guilt kicks in they start to feel bad and move to an inner language where it has all failed. This then gives them permission to stop the change process and revert in full to the previous state. The trick is to help the client learn how to (a) just admit they have made a mistake and (b) reflect on what can be learned from the slippage. This way it can be seen as simply a small blip and not a reason to backslide.

Coaching questions

Heart buckets	▪ What emotional triggers will make you feel like giving up? ▪ What negative emotions do you tend to experience when attempting difficult things?
Head buckets	▪ What triggers make you think about giving up? ▪ What inner language do you hear yourself saying when things go wrong? ▪ What triggers you to think negative thoughts?
Hand buckets	▪ What triggers prompt negative behaviours? ▪ Do you have any habits that surface when under pressure? ▪ How would I recognize behaviours that indicate a reversion to the old ways?
Heart balloons	▪ What can you do to improve how you feel? ▪ What can others do that might make you feel better? ▪ How have you got rid of negative emotions in the past?
Head balloons	▪ What helps to get rid of negative thoughts? ▪ What can others do to help get rid of negative autopilots? ▪ How have you got rid of them in the past?
Hand balloons	▪ What helps to get rid of negative behaviours? ▪ What can others do to help get rid of negative habits? ▪ How have you got rid of them in the past?

Climb Miracle Mountain

Nothing contributes so much to tranquilizing the mind as a steady purpose – a point on which the soul may fix its intellectual eye.

Mary Wollstonecraft Shelley

One of the risks with any personal change process is that people look for and accept the simpler, cheaper and quicker solution without understanding that sustainable change often requires modification at a much deeper level. We all look for the quick fix, the easy buck and the miracle solution that will solve our problem in the blink of an eye. This is so often characterized by the overdependence on pills for ills rather than accepting that sustainable personal change requires hard work and real effort on the part of the client. For example, look at these various quick-fix solutions:

> **❝ We all look for the quick fix, the easy buck and the miracle solution. ❞**

a) Weight – hunger suppression pills.

b) Drink – change to coke.

c) Health – food replacements.

d) Leadership skills – the 'learn how to smile more' course.

e) Attraction to opposite sex – new clothes.

f) Time management – new diary system.

g) Improve a difficult relationship – go on holiday.

However, maybe like me your solutions might look like:

a) Weight – hunger suppression pills – drop 6lb – think it is cracked so drift back to bad foods.

b) Drink – change to coke – all goes well until mate's birthday party – then try just a few beers.

c) Health – food replacements – seem fine – but soon tire of boring supplements and desire for real food kicks in.

d) Leadership skills – The 'learn how to smile more' course – get fed up with being the 'nice' boss and revert to screaming autocrat once one of the team really messes up.

e) Attraction to opposite sex – new clothes – feel good for a while – but then paranoia sets in about funny-looking nose or complexion.

f) Time management – new diary system – looks really good on the shelf – and stays there!

g) Improve a difficult relationship – go on holiday – and argue every day.

The common problem with all of these solutions is that the client is looking for extrinsic factors to resolve what are inherently intrinsic problems. Problems in a relationship are basically about the shared desire and purpose of the people to make it work, even in the hard times. It is not about the surrounding artefacts and environment. Although they may well influence how the relationship performs, at heart it is about understanding the deep factors that drive and underpin how people relate. Hence we need to help the client take a holistic view to the coaching process – to understand all the forces that impact on their ability to effect sustainable personal change.

This can be aided by using a taxonomic structure that identifies how different levels of change can be enacted. The five key changes that the client can make to their life are:

1 Property – get a new fixed asset, product or piece of equipment.

2 Process – change how something is being managed.

3 Proficiency – acquire new skills.

4 Passion – gain more motivation.

5 Purpose – understand why it is important and fits with life goals.

The model is called Miracle Mountain (Figure 11.6) because if someone really does fix a deep intrinsic problem such as a lack of self-worth, depression or being under-motivated by simply getting a new car or doing things differently, then it might well be a miracle. It can happen, but where these types of issues are deep-seated it will be quite rare and very unethical of the coach to allow the client to think that a new tie will instantly make them more attractive to the opposite sex!

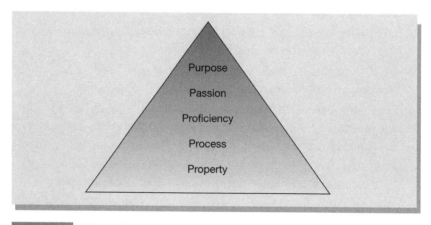

Figure 11.6   Miracle Mountain

If the root of the intrinsic problem can be traced back to the personal sense of passion and purpose, it behoves the coach to ensure that the client has climbed the mountain to try to address these issues as part of the solution. But climbing Miracle Mountain can be a hard and long task as people are not used to looking inside and truly discovering and sharing who they are and why certain things are important to them.

One of the first things a coach needs to determine when meeting a client is where on the model the root cause is coming from. Consider the manager who is having time management problems. They are missing meetings, not hitting deadlines and being perceived as not ready for promotion because they are not under control. They come to the coach desperate for help and to find a way to resolve the problem. As part of the early debate the coach should be seeking to ask questions around the five levels to understand where the root cause might be. The five areas that the coach is testing can be seen in Figure 11.7.

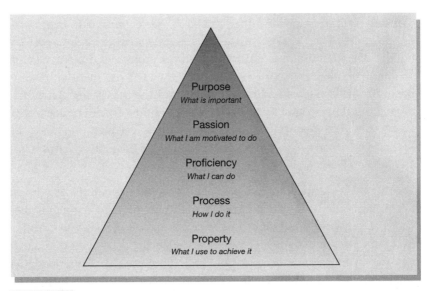

Figure 11.7   Miracle Mountain parameters

With this we are seeking to understand the person in relation to the perceived problem. The key areas being tested are:

■ Property: What tools and systems are currently used to manage your time?

■ Process: How do you manage your time at present?

- Proficiency: Do you have the necessary time management skills and capability?
- Passion: Why do you really want to manage your time?
- Purpose: Why is this so important now?

The problem with many time management solutions and training programmes is they focus overly on the bottom two levels (here is a diary and schedule to use it) but pay little attention to the person's ability to use such tools: why they want to manage their time and what is important to them.

In many (maybe most) cases it is the top two levels that deserve the most attention but get the least focus. Taking the time management case, we should accept as a principle that the choices someone makes are the right choices for them at that moment in time. So when someone chooses to meet a friend for dinner rather than spend time updating their diary, it is because at that moment in time they are motivated to take that action (passion) because in reality their friend is more important than work (purpose). They might say that the time management is more important, but the behaviour indicates otherwise. Now the problem is that this passion and purpose often sit in a deep shadow that they will not share with others because they have to be perceived to do and say the right thing. But at that moment in time, when faced with the choice point of friend or diary, they choose friend; the person who says they want to get promotion can't be bothered to attend the new management course; or the non-smoker has just one more to be sociable.

Looking at the choice point in more detail, we understand that it was driven by an emotional sense that it would be fun, then the inner autopilot voice said that they were owed some time off as a treat and the hand just instinctively went out and dialled the number. The crucial point with this is that no matter what system the course or coach has given the client, no matter what processes are in place, and possibly no matter how proficient they are at managing their diary, this passion and purpose will in most cases override the lower three drivers and negate all the work invested in those three levels (Figure 11.8).

This is the decay that we see so often with management training courses, personal development programmes, and college study programmes. It can even be seen where people decide that because they are unhappy the solution is a 'place in the sun'. They find the villa (property), understand the route by which they can purchase it and maybe live in the area (process),

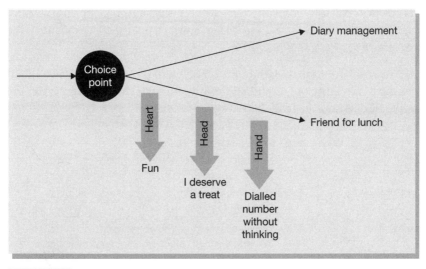

Figure 11.8   Choice point forces

learn a smattering of the language (proficiency), only to find that when they get there they are not really motivated to work in the sun (passion), or they don't like mingling with the locals because the culture is so different and emphasis in placed on things that are not important to them (purpose). This pseudo-miracle solution is prevalent in all areas of personal change and is one that causes immense misery for the client and upset for the coach.

I really do believe that whether in coaching, training or any life-changing or development action these two aspects are absolutely critical to ensuring that a sustainable change is realized. Purpose and passion lead to performance and payback – people who have both purpose and passion for an event will create sustainable value for themselves and the sponsoring organization. People who attend an event without both clear purpose and motivation can waste their time, disrupt the learning process for others and potentially degrade the overall programme through negative feedback after the event.

> **❝ Purpose and passion lead to performance and payback. ❞**

If these two aspects are in place (either at the outset of the partnership or as a consequence of the coach's actions), we can begin to understand how the Miracle Mountain questions can help deliver a sustainable change. As a basic proposition I tend to believe that all five levels will need to be considered for any coaching engagement. Even if no action needs to be taken (for example, someone has all the necessary property and physical assets to make a change), the coach must challenge to ensure that the necessary aspects are in place.

If we consider the client with time management problems, the coach might consider (from the outset and all the way through the coaching cycle) the types of questions in Table 11.3.

Table 11.3 Questions for time management problems

Mountain level	Question types
5 Purpose	■ What is wrong with your current approach? ■ What will the change mean to you?
4 Passion	■ Why is this important to you now? ■ Is there anything else more important than this at the moment?
3 Proficiency	■ What skills do you have to manage your time? ■ What skills do you see in other people who can manage their time?
2 Process	■ How do you currently manage your time? What process do you follow? ■ Have you seen other processes that might be better or worse?
1 Property	■ What system do you have? ■ How practical is it in terms of portability and practicability of use?

By addressing the top three levels the coach is beginning to address the intrinsic issues and not just focus on the extrinsic issues covered on the first two levels. By tackling both issues there is a greater chance that the coach will be able to close the coaching engagement with confidence that the client will be self-sufficient and that reversion will not occur.

Coaching questions

5 Purpose
■ Why is this important to you?
■ What is wrong with your current approach?
■ What will the change mean to you?

4 Passion
■ Why is this important to you now?
■ What would happen if you didn't make a change?
■ Is there anything else more important than this at the moment?

3 Proficiency ■ What skills do you have to manage this?

■ What skills do you see in other people who can manage this?

■ What skills do you see lacking in people who don't seem to manage this?

2 Process ■ How do you currently manage this? What process do you follow?

■ How would you critique the way you work?

■ Have you seen other processes that might be better or worse?

1 Property ■ What systems do you have?

■ What tools do you use?

■ Where does it happen? Is this important?

John's journey

Two months into the coaching process John was feeling really good. He had built a good network of people who were happy to help with his journey and felt that he had developed great relationship-building skills. However, Julie wanted to help him think about what would happen once the coaching process was complete.

Buckets and balloons

After talking it through they concluded that one of the primary buckets would come once he started out on his own. If work was light he worried that he might begin to panic and network from a selfish rather than a shared position. If this happened his peers could see him as selfish and so erode the network.

In talking it through with Julie he planned to use the cockpit measurement tool to watch for signs of emotional anxiety and negative autopilots. He felt that it would be possible to counterbalance this by ensuring that he found a few close colleagues in the network with whom he could share the negative thoughts and feelings and so diffuse them before he could go into a spiral.

Now John had tasted the new life Julie wanted to ensure that it was one that he really wanted and was not just a flaky dream. She took John through Miracle Mountain and asked him to build two versions of the mountain: one for the old John and one for the new John. She wanted him to really think through the difference in his life on all the levels and appreciate how much of a gap there might be between the two. By under-

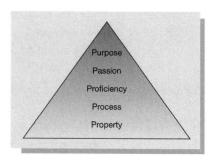

Miracle Mountain

standing the potential difference and the corresponding choices that would be needed she hoped it would help him to confirm that it would be sustainable and he wouldn't drift back after a few months.

This exercise helped John because it really made him appreciate in tangible terms the difference between what he was and what he wanted to be. Moreover, it confirmed that the pull towards the new was far greater than the rubber band that might pull him back.

12

Close – flying solo

The story so far

The client and coach have developed an understanding of the current situation and the perfect picture. Solutions have been identified, deployed, and measurements have been established. Where the client has slipped from their planned journey the coach has helped them to get back in line, and they have also developed strategies to maintain their journey when slippage occurs. The coach will now work with the client to bring the engagement to a close and help ensure that they are ready to fly solo.

Enter the Close stage

Coaching relationships begin, grow, but must eventually end. If they don't then they are not coaching – they are probably management. However, the danger is that because it is the tail end of the process it becomes all too easy to minimize or negate the process. It can too easily become 'let's have a quick chat over coffee' or 'I will give you a call later'. The Close stage deserves a great deal more effort than this for a number of reasons:

- It is a chance to celebrate success, for both the coach and client.
- It offers the client time and space to reflect and look back over the process to see what they have learned.
- It signals to other stakeholders that the process is over.
- It provides a finite and symbolic break for the client to walk away.
- For personal or private coaches it might be the point of final billing and maybe a bonus!

Although there are a number of tools to consider and apply at the Close stage, the two covered here are related to the need to review both the learning and the final outcome of the process, together with the need to ensure that the client can fly solo and is not dependent on the coach for any further support.

Look back and learn

If you don't know where you are going, you will probably end up somewhere else.

Laurence J. Peter

The coach is responsible in partnership with the client for ensuring not just that the job is done but also that the desired value was achieved, why it worked and how the client can learn from the experience. To do this a key component in the Close stage is the ability to learn and reflect on what actually happened.

The After Action Review (AAR) is a powerful tool that can assist you with managing this process. It does this by eliciting feedback under a relatively controlled process. Typically both coach and client will take time out to examine in a non-judgemental way whether the anticipated value was realized, how the engagement was managed and any learning points, and suggest ways that the next engagement might be improved.

The whole AAR process is meant to be simple so that it can be conducted with ease in any situation. The essence of the model is to follow a set of five primary questions (Figure 12.1):

1 **What value did we seek to deliver?**
   - What was the objective at the outset of the engagement?
   - Did we have a clear outcome?
   - Were the players in the change clear?
   - Were the measures communicated and understood?
   - What are the different perceptions from each member of the review?

2 **What value did we deliver?**
   - What was the outcome?
   - How do we know?
   - What does each person perceive to be the outcome and what are the perception gaps?
   - What explicit evidence do we have?
   - What anecdotal or intangible evidence do we have?

3 What helped to create value and what didn't help?

- Was there any gap between what we expected to happen and what actually happened?
- How would we rate the outcome against our expectations and the client's expectations?
- What helped the good to be good?
- What caused the bad to be bad?
- What helped the success or caused the failure?
- What alternative courses of actions might have been more effective?

4 What have we learned?

- What would we do differently next time?
- How would this add value?
- What would we do more of next time?
- What would we do less of?
- Have we received any insight from comments made by others while on the journey?

5 What should we take forward to use next time?

- How can we use what we have learned with this in a future partnership?
- How can we also use it in our professional or personal life?

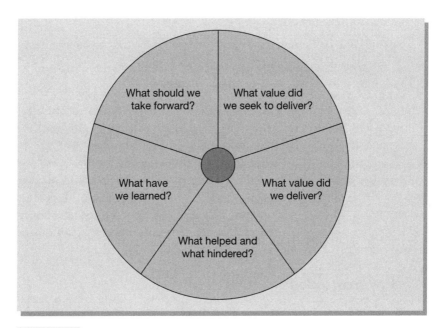

Figure12.1   Look and learn wheel

The important thing about this stage is that it seeks to create a safe container, where the client is able to truly express what their thoughts and feelings are about the coaching exercise and not worry about hurting the other's feelings. Now, it would be foolish to think that this can always be guaranteed because people are people – but the use of a formal agenda and structure with defined ground rules about behaviour and desired outcomes goes a long way towards facilitating an open learning process. Part of the key is that it should always seek to deal with fact and avoid the danger of subjective judgement (fantasies). If the review begins to focus on blame rather than what objectively occurred then it is probably heading down a spiral and that will kill any chance for real, tangible learning.

The primary benefits at this stage will be that it:

- creates a pause point where both the client and coach can take a breath;

- allows the client to test intended against actual outcomes;

- allows for triangulation of data – by pulling together different sources into a single review process;

- identifies what to keep, what to let go and what to amplify next time round;

- links the three threads of operation, tactical and strategic change under a single review process;

- captures and communicates learning based on fact rather than fantasy;

- signals a deep desire on the part of the coach and client to learn and to take this learning into future change processes.

The closure process might be viewed as both an art and a science. The art is in the coach's ability to create a thick trust relationship along the coaching journey so that by the end the client feels able to share their true thoughts and feelings about the process. The science is in the ability to manage the closure process so that it doesn't become a random walk or just another casual conversation. It must have purpose and passion if the reflective process is to offer any significant value.

> **❝ The closure process might be viewed as both an art and a science. ❞**

Coaching questions

- What was your perfect picture at the outset?

- Have you achieved it?

■ How do you know it has been achieved?

■ Is there any gap between what you expected and what you achieved?

■ What helped the success or caused the failure?

■ What would you do differently next time?

■ Can we use what we have learned with this in a future partnership?

Fly solo

Self-reliance is the only road to true freedom, and being one's own person is its ultimate reward.

Patricia Sampson

All through the coaching journey the coach is working to grow the relationship so that they develop a high degree of trust and responsiveness with the client. However, as this relationship grows, so can the level of dependence between the coach and client. Think about any loving relationship in your life – the closer you get, the greater the level of dependence that can emerge. The problem is that at the end of the day, both you and the client have to let go and break away from the coaching relationship. The onus is on you as the coach to ensure that at the point of departure all unnecessary levels of dependence have gone from the relationship so that the client is able to fly solo with confidence.

When the coaching relationship begins, the coach is often seen as 'the expert', someone who has all the right answers and will be able to help resolve the problem. While this can help to ensure that buy-in takes place, the danger is that a dependent relationship is formed – one where the client is sometimes unwilling to let go of your perceived expertise. This is seen in the patient who will only go to see one particular doctor or the preference that you might have for a particular car mechanic. However, a problem can arise when the doctor or mechanic decides to move. You are left high and dry, without anywhere to turn when the next problem surfaces. There is a difficult balance in any client relationship. The coach must be close enough to develop a trust-based association, but distant enough to allow independence and freedom.

❝You are left high and dry, without anywhere to turn when the next problem surfaces.❞

Although not seen in all coaching relationships, a common pattern is shown in Figure 12.2. This is how the dependency changes over time as the coach and client go round the 7Cs framework. The first stage is where the coach meets the client. There is still a freedom of choice about the relationship, like a couple out on a first date sizing each other up. Once there is an agreement that a relationship will be formed, the coach will be quite dependent on the client as they need them to open up and deliver passion and purpose to ensure that a sustainable outcome is achieved. Once the process moves into the create and change stage, there is a shared dependency – both parties have invested time and reputation in the relationship and cannot afford to see it fail. Once beyond this, the coach is probably confident about the chances for sustainable change and might well be starting to think about moving towards closure. However, now the client has a strong dependency on the coach as they have been there all along to ease the pain and light the way ahead. At the final stage, both coach and client should be back at the start of the loop, able to reflect on the relationship in the cold light of day. It is from this rational position that any decision is taken to pursue further options for working together.

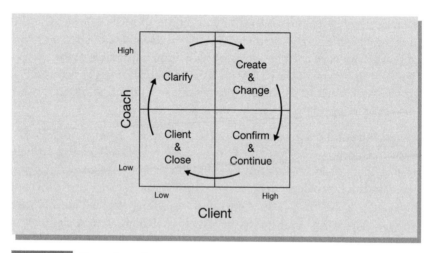

Figure 12.2   Dependency journey

Problems can arise where the coach seeks to close the relationship while the client is still dependent on them. Coaching partnerships often have problems because the coach has gone and the client is left high and dry without the real confidence or ability to run with the change. As a result, one of several things can happen:

■ The client reverts to the state that existed at the outset of the partnership.

▪ The client asks the coach to return and fix some of the problems again.

▪ The client turns against the coach and employs a different firm to fix the problems.

Whatever option is followed, the end result is unsatisfactory and one that should be avoided. Dependence is a positive state only when both parties are aware of the condition. If one or both parties are unaware of the reliance, this can only lead to an unhealthy situation. Your goal is to develop a relationship that is based upon a spirit of mutual interdependence.

The key to this is often a process of managed withdrawal. The coach should ensure that the client appreciates the importance of dependence-free partnership from the outset. Once the language of dependence, independence and flying solo is embedded, this should be used consciously throughout the engagement. As the engagement progresses the coach should move from using the language of independence to putting the client in a position where they have to demonstrate independence. Finally, as the journey progresses round to the closing stage the coach should back right off and ensure that the client is flying solo and can demonstrate their independence.

For example, when running a 7Cs training course, I will seek to build a relationship with the group and work to answer and resolve any issues they might have. This could be a question related to the course or it might be replenishing coffee that is cold or dealing with rooms that are too hot. As the course progresses I will consciously do two things. First, I will seek to not answer questions and encourage the group to resolve issues from within. Second, I will look for evidence that the group is beginning to own the learning. One clear indication of this comes when they choose to change my direction on how to manage a particular exercise. If when walking round the room delegates begin to say they have modified the process because it aids their learning, that is a clear sign that they are beginning to fly solo. Finally, towards the end of the programme, I again do two things. First, I refuse to answer any questions about the course content and instead challenge people to get their solutions from other people in the room. Second, I explain to the group what I am doing and why I am doing it. This way we are able to talk about the nature of dependence and how part of my role is to not answer their questions, even when they express a real need. In this way I am trying to manage the withdrawal process, but to do it in a way that is open, honest and discussable.

Testing for readiness

The final stage of the coaching process is for the coach to have absolute confidence that the client is ready to fly solo. When I asked three colleagues who teach people to fly how they knew when someone was ready to end the coaching relationship, their answer could be summarized as follows:

- **Capability:** Have the coach's instructions been practised and successfully followed through so that the student will not do anything silly and wreck the plane?

- **Belief:** Has the student absorbed the key messages?

- **Attitude:** Can the student demonstrate confidence in their ability and are not too cocky?

- **Tested:** Has the student completed the mandatory elements before soloing – engine fail after take-off training, etc.?

- **Responsiveness:** Would the student be able to cope with the home airfield runway having to close due to an unexpected occurrence?

The final assurance that the pilot can fly solo is for them to fly solo. The ultimate test is to brief them thoroughly on what to do (just one circuit and a full stop landing, nothing fancy or clever). Then let them fly and watch the flight from the ground so that you can give feedback. Finally, can they do three good landings in a row?

What fascinated me about these comments were (a) the similarity in responses – there seems to be a consistent view across three disparate people who were involved in some way in coaching or being coached to fly; and (b) how the measures of readiness to fly solo can be linked back to where we started with the coaching framework, i.e. the Heart, Head and Hand model. Which ultimately seems to make sense.

For me the final test of readiness can be mapped across the 3D model outlined in the Client stage and seen in Figure 12.3. With this the coach and client should seek to self-test and assure themselves that all is ready for take-off, to ensure that the client has competence and confidence in their ability to go out and not return to the coach for assistance at a later date.

> **❝ The final test of readiness can be mapped across the 3D model outlined in the Client stage. ❞**

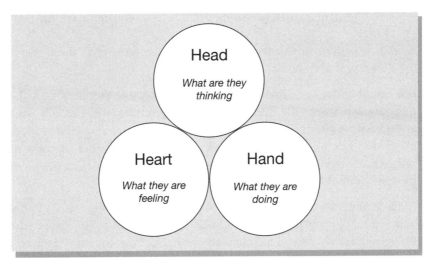

Figure 12.3 3D model

The key areas they will seek to assure themselves of might include:

■ **Heart:**
  - A sense of displayed confidence.
  - A feeling of assurance within themselves.
  - No shift towards the Stressed or Sad quadrant on the e-Map when under pressure.
  - An ability to take pleasure in the new process.
  - Not being over-confident and recognizing that some fear can be useful.

■ **Head:**
  - Does not use negative or doubtful inner language.
  - Does not use negative or doubtful language to others.
  - Can visualize and describe what good looks like.
  - Might be aware of any potentially dangerous assumptions that are embedded, but has strategies to avoid or compensate for them.
  - Aware of any deep fears that might impact the ability to fly solo.
  - Aware of creep or reversion that has occurred in previous change process and how that impacted sustainability of outcomes.

■ **Hand:**
  - Has been able to let go of old habits and behaviours.
  - New behaviours are embedded and comfortable.
  - Can describe new skills and behaviours and how they are being applied.

- Can recognize when behavioural slippage or reversion starts to occur.
- Can perform any behavioural tests that are necessary as part of the new way of working.

It is important to note that this is not something that you do just in the measurement stage. The pilot teaching a novice flyer will be doing this assessment from day one and the manager preparing someone for promotion will do this from the point that someone says that are ready to progress. These measures commence in the Client stage and the assessment process continues all the way through the coaching journey.

I finally understood the importance of this ongoing and continual closure when trying to obtain my motorbike licence. As an ageing biker, the thought of taking a test filled me with dread. But I can honestly say it was one of the most stimulating experiences in my life. However, the process the motorcycle coaches put me through was really interesting. The big thing was that I thought I went there to pass the test, but they were coaching me to ride a bike safely.

My first confusion came after a few days when we shifted from riding the 125cc to the bigger 500cc bikes. Up until then we had ridden around town, tracing the test route and getting to feel comfortable with the bikes. However, when we shifted to the bigger bikes they started driving out into the wilds of Essex and encouraging us to open up the bikes – and even worse, open them up round the corners. Although this was a great experience, I keep thinking, 'So what has this got to do with my test?' However, after I passed (luckily), the penny finally dropped as I realized that they were playing a much deeper game than I had understood. Their goal (I believe) was to address the Heart and Head dimensions as well as the Hand. Anyone can physically ride a bike, but safety comes from confidence on the road (Heart) and the ability to keep a clear head and eliminate self-doubt (Head). By pushing us to go beyond our expectation they were helping to build up confidence and dispose of any doubt about our ability to deal with unpredictable cars and corners. By the time we took the test, it seemed like a piece of cake in comparison with the exploits we had been undertaking during the previous few days. It was this investment in these dimensions and the structured constant assessment of what we were doing, feeling and saying that helped them to help me pass the test. (Thanks, guys.)

Coaching questions

Reduced dependence	■ Is there anything else you need from me?
	■ How could you prove to me that I am not needed any more?
	■ What would prove to others that you are independent from me?
Heart test	■ Now that you have flown solo for a while, how did it feel?
	■ Is it what you expected?
	■ Would you like to experience any other feelings?
Head test	■ Now that you have flown solo for a while, what are you thinking?
	■ Is it what you expected?
	■ Would you like to experience any other thoughts?
	■ What improvements do you need to make next?
	■ Could you teach what you have learned to someone else?
	■ What is the big lesson you would share with others about your journey?
Hand test	■ Now that you have flown solo for a while, what new capabilities do you have?
	■ Is it what you expected?
	■ Would you like to develop any further capabilities?

John's journey

Once John had developed a robust network, this gave him an awareness of the earning potential in his chosen market, the capabilities he would need to develop and a confidence that he would be able to prosper as a personal coach.

Julie and John agreed that the time had come for them to move on, so they went into the review stage. They decided to manage this in a slightly different way. Rather than doing a face-to-face review, each of them made an audio recording that covered the question tackled in the look back and learn phase.

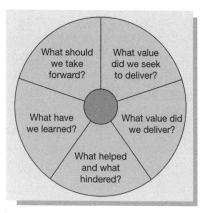

Look and learn

Julie asked John to do this for two reasons. First, it gave them time to be really reflective and hopefully surface learning in a very selfish way. Second, it continued and helped to complete the process maintained through the journey of ensuring that John does not become over-dependent on Julie. By making him build his personal learning case study he could not use her as a crutch to elicit the learning.

Once they had listened to each other's tapes they then looked for areas of shared learning and from this they were able to build a rich picture of the process and the learning from it.

More importantly, Julie and John were able to ensure that they had been able to deliver the agreed change and outcome that was contracted at the outset of the engagement.

The final test was whether John could fly solo. Would he be able to continue and progress without Julie's support? To test this they decided to have some fun. The test of John's ability to prosper would be crystallized in his ability to manage micro-moments, the three-minute gap between meeting someone new and building a relationship with them. To test this Julie and John went to a shopping mall where Julie sat in a coffee shop and just watched John approach people with his business card.

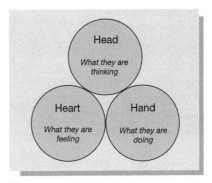

Fly solo

After an hour of watching him 'perform' she felt really sure that John, the self-conscious engineer, had blossomed into a confident person who was proud of his abilities and able to sell them. She felt proud of the fact that she had helped John to deliver a personal change that would stand the test of time and at no point in the engagement had she needed to tell him what to do or how to do it.

13

Putting it into action

Once you have a reasonable understanding of the underlying philosophy behind the Collaborative Coaching framework, and some of the core tools, the next step is obviously to give it a try. As you begin to use the framework try to bear in mind some of the following ideas, as they will make the whole process smoother and more successful. The ideas in this final section are not about the framework itself but more about a few tips and ideas for putting into practice.

Coaching contracting

I would really love to be able to offer the definitive, all-encompassing outline contract that can be used in any coaching engagement. The trouble is that I don't believe such a thing exists. I could quite happily give you a nice list of contractual elements that should be included, but all coaching engagements are driven by such a rich array of variables (Figure 13.1):

- The content of the coaching topic.
- The context where the coaching is taking place (work, sports, etc.).
- The competence of the clients (prior knowledge of the process) and the competence of the coach.
- Your confidence in them (prior experience and level of trust fund) and their confidence in you.
- The extent to which a commercial or financial interest is involved for services provided.

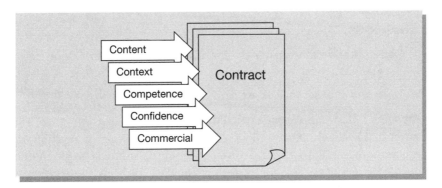

Figure 13.1   Some contractual elements

Hence, because of the potential variability in these areas it can be difficult to establish a standard model. All that the coach and client can do is to consider the need for a contract (explicit or implicit) and work to find a process and model that suits both players.

The should consider the following:

- **Objectives:** What is the desired outcome of the engagement?
- **Measurement:** How will the outcome be demonstrated?
- **Timeframe:** When is it to be closed?
- **Approach:** What coaching approach framework will be followed?
- **Resource allocation:** How much time do both players need to allocate?
- **Key breakpoints:** What must be achieved and by when?
- **Responsibilities:** What is each person responsible for in the relationship?
- **Others:** Are there any other stakeholders who have an interest in the process and outcome?
- **Exclusion:** Are there any specific areas the client or coach do not wish to deal with?
- **Potential risks:** What could go wrong and how will this be resolved?
- **Payment:** What are the terms and conditions?
- **Termination process:** Is there right of termination of the partnership and are there any penalties?
- **Liability:** Does the client need to express their liability policy?

- **Confidentiality:** Are there boundaries of confidentiality to be observed?

- **Renegotiation strategy:** What if things change because of the impact of external factors?

- **Review:** What are the closure dates?

Remember that the contract should never include anything that will surprise the client. If the client observes a new item, proposition or assumption, trust will be eroded. If you or the client cannot be trusted at the opening stages of the relationship, what chance is there that integrity will be maintained if the relationship hits turbulent waters?

In developing the contract, it is important to remember that it is a framework for the delivery of a service or product. It is not being written as a stick for either party to beat the other. If the contract reads like a 'screw-down' document, there is every chance that the relationship will operate according to those principles. If it is written with the intention that it will not see the light of day until the process is complete, there will be a greater chance that the relationship will operate with a collaborative spirit. However, before the contract is written, many of the details contained within the document must be negotiated, and this is where problems can surface.

> **❝ The goal at the contract stage must be to take extra care in the specification of the desired outcomes. ❞**

As the old adage goes, 'measure twice, cut once'. The goal at the contract stage must be to take extra care in the specification of the desired outcomes. This must be in the criteria specified in the document and more especially in the allocation of roles and responsibilities between you and the client. One of the biggest causes of downstream problems can be disagreement over who owns what action or who is responsible for a particular aspect of the change. Simply by locking in clarity at this stage it is possible to minimize any problems that might occur at a later date.

Rapid mapping

It is amazing to think about how many important things are decided in the first ten minutes of meeting the client:

- The nature of the relationship and whether there is mutual respect in the professionalism of both players.

■ Whether the coach wants to take on the client's project.

■ Whether the client wants to use the coach.

■ Whether the proposed change has life, will survive and can add value for both players.

■ What level of risk entering into a coaching partnership exposes to both players.

The problem is that both players need to ascertain this type of information before committing to any type of formal relationship, but this can be difficult under time pressure. The client is keen to resolve the issue fast because it is causing them a problem. The coach is being (subtley) pressured to take on the client because they need to hit the company utilization targets, fill the diary, or earn some revenue. As a consequence the first coaching date often looks like the first romantic encounter: both players eager to meet and get to know each other, while at the same time having a pre-arranged escape path just in case it doesn't feel right. The trouble is that a successful kiss on a first date is not a good predictor of a long-term relationship. In the same way, the early coffee chat offers little chance for either side to really ascertain whether the coaching relationship will enable both sides to create real value from the engagement.

The 7Cs life cycle framework is quite deliberately not a complex model. As such it can be used in a very short timeframe to produce a rich and robust understanding of the client's situation without attempting to climb into the detail or resolve the problem too quickly. This allows the coach to determine whether they wish to pursue the relationship, the client to determine whether they wish to work with the coach and both players to rapidly ascertain whether the project is worth pursuing.

The rapid mapping technique allows you to spin the client around the 7Cs framework in 10–15 minutes (Figure 13.2). The goal is not to climb inside the situation or define a solution; it is simply to understand the client's perception of the problem and make a conscious choice about whether to proceed to the next stage of the engagement. It's the same as when you are buying a new car. You will ascertain a number of key points about the person and the car over the telephone or via e-mail. If at this stage you feel comfortable that the sale is viable and of value, you might be prepared to commit a few hours to drive to their house to have a look in more detail.

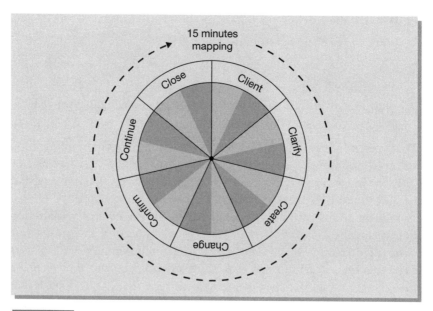

Figure 13.2 7Cs framework in 15 minutes

The coaching process is often no different. The potential client might call you up, meet you in a corridor, or simply pop in as they are passing the office. At that stage they may outline the problem they are trying to resolve. This stage is normally quite rushed as both client and coach are in the middle of something else, so it is literally time for coffee and a croissant.

Hence all you might have time for is to ask the following questions:

■ **CLIENT:**
- How would you like the future to be different from today?
- Why do you need outside help to make this happen?
- What is the 'specific' change you require?
- What value can I add?

■ **CLARIFY:**
- Is the change based on fact or intuition?
- Are there any areas that you would not be happy talking about with me?
- What is stopping you from doing this already and are you prepared to share this with me?
- Are you sure that your assumptions about the issue are not biased or clouded?

▪ **CREATE:**
  - Have you thought about the criteria for a good solution?
  - Do you have a solution already in mind and are you prepared to look at alternative options?
  - Do you want to be creative or practical when developing the solution?
  - What role would I play in the creative process?

▪ **CHANGE:**
  - Are you prepared to let go of the past?
  - What resistance might you have in letting go of entrenched habits?
  - What might you find difficult about making the change?
  - How might you work through any difficult stages?

▪ **CONFIRM:**
  - How do you know there is a problem?
  - What evidence do you have?
  - Do others share your belief that there is a problem?
  - How will you know when it has been resolved?

▪ **CONTINUE:**
  - Have previous changes that you have attempted failed to last?
  - What are the triggers that might cause you to revert to old habits?
  - What might cause slippage or reversion?
  - What factors will help it last?

▪ **CLOSE:**
  - When complete, how will things be different for you?
  - What problems might you have in maintaining the change once complete?
  - Will you be dependent on anyone to make it last?
  - What value will the change add?

At this stage you have briefly spun the client around the 7Cs framework and should have enough data to make a go or no-go decision. If you can get round the seven stages and come away both knowing and feeling that the engagement can be delivered, will add value and will be sustainable, the chances are that it is worth progressing to the next stage. If, however, you touch some roadblocks (explicit or implicit), you still have the option to decline the invitation. Although you might not wish to reject potential client engagements, you might have cause for concern if the client says the following as you progress round the rapid mapping process, as seen in Figure 13.3:

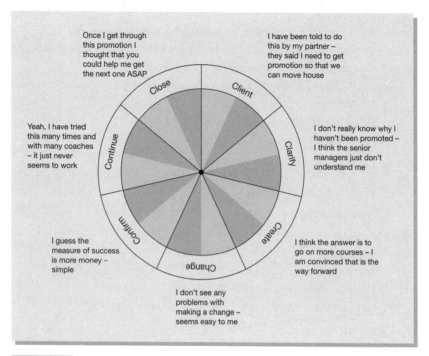

Once I get through this promotion I thought that you could help me get the next one ASAP

I have been told to do this by my partner – they said I need to get promotion so that we can move house

Yeah, I have tried this many times and with many coaches – it just never seems to work

I don't really know why I haven't been promoted – I think the senior managers just don't understand me

I guess the measure of success is more money – simple

I think the answer is to go on more courses – I am convinced that is the way forward

I don't see any problems with making a change – seems easy to me

Close *Client* *Clarify* *Create* *Change* *Confirm* *Continue*

Figure 13.3   Rapid mapping responses

One of the more practical benefits of the rapid mapping process is that the client cannot fail to be impressed with your professionalism. Within 15 minutes you will have demonstrated:

- that you understand what makes successful coaching work;
- the ability to use a simple framework tool to investigate and understand a problem, even within a limited timeframe;
- that where necessary you can analyze with clarity and not bluster and bluff through the use of complex concepts that no one can understand;
- to the client any possible areas of risk that they might not have considered or understood prior to the conversation.

However, the most important aspect is by sending signals of your integrity and professionalism the chances are that the client will be more than willing to move to the next stage of the engagement which would be to ask you to meet with them for a full review to consider the project in more detail.

Client pre-work

As already mentioned, one of the problems with coaching can be in the implicit transfer of the problem from client to coach. When people have a problem it is too easy to go to the coach in the expectation that they will wave a magic wand and solve the problem. The trouble is that the coach has no miracle cure. All they have is a process to help you make sense of the problem yourself. Coaching is simply about *helping people to help themselves*. Helping themselves is the definitive part of the statement.

ff Coaching is simply about *helping people* to help themselves. 55

Since this is the case, it makes sense for the client to begin the 'help yourself' before they see the coach. Coaching is a collaborative relationship: you get out what you put in. So if the client is serious about making a sustainable change, they will get serious about undertaking the necessary preparatory work. That way when they meet the coach they will be more inclined to take the client seriously and invest the necessary time and energy to resolve the issue.

People who believe they can benefit from coaching should first embark on a short journey of self-discovery. In this journey they will ask a number of questions of themselves in relation to coaching and draw a number of conclusions they might not have considered previously.

The client questions

The coach gives these questions to the client before agreeing to a new coaching partnership. For example, the client might decide that they want help in gaining promotion because the last three interviews haven't worked out very well. In this case the coach might spend a short time with them to understand the background, but would not seek to climb inside the issue or consider how to resolve the problem. Once they have a feel for the problem and what the client wants to achieve, then they may ask the client to take away a set of questions to consider ready for the next meeting.

Table 13.1 sets out the basic form of the pre-coaching question. Although there are variations, this gives the basic backbone of the question that the coach should encourage the client to address before engaging fully in the relationship.

Table 13.1	The basic form of the pre-coaching question

Questions

CLIENT

1a) **Why do I want coaching, why now, and why with this coach? What can the coach do that I can't already do for myself?**

Are you really serious about addressing the issue or is the need for a coach simply a way to transfer the problem on to someone else's shoulders? What specific value do you want the coach to give? If you don't know, then how will they?

1b) **What is the change I want to make and how will it deliver value for me?**

If you can't be specific about the outcome you want then you will enter the coaching session looking woolly and vague. Hence much of the time will be spent going round in circles trying to understand exactly what you want to achieve.

CLARIFY

2a) **What is stopping me from doing this already?**

Most coaching sessions are about helping the person take their foot off the brake rather than putting their foot on the accelerator. People generally have all the resources they need to achieve what they want – they just don't know or believe it.

2b) **Can I be sure that my assumptions about the issue are not biased or clouded?**

We all have maps of the world that are clouded and corrupted. Clouded by laziness and a unwillingness to look beyond the horizon. Corrupted because we believe the stories that our friends, newspapers and television tell us. Much of the coaching process is about stripping away these false horizons and getting a clear and focused picture of what is going on.

CREATE

3a) **Do I have a hidden solution already in mind and am I really prepared to look at alternative options?**

Many people meet the coach with a predefined solution in mind. They might not voice it at the first meeting, but it is there. An example of this might be, I am unhappy (the answer is a villa in Spain) or I am overweight (the answer is a diet).

3b) **Have I thought through the criteria for a successful solution?**

Too often solution generation takes place without understanding the criteria for a good solution. It always pays to consider time (when do I need it by?), cost (can I afford it?) and quality (how perfect does it need to be?).

Table 13.1   Continued

Questions

CHANGE

4a) What might I find difficult about making the change?

All change is about letting go of the old and accepting a new way of thinking, feeling and behaving. However, as human beings we tend not to like this and prefer to stay in the same old slippers or comfy chair. This seeks to question just what difficulties will surface with the letting go and whether you are prepared to deal with them.

4b) How might the coach help me through any difficult stages?

At some point when preparing for your first marathon you may not want to get out of bed. Does the coach get you out (and so begin the addiction of dependency) or do they let you stay in bed and deal with the problem on your own (with a risk that you might give up altogether)? The level and type of intervention that you want and need must be considered.

CONFIRM

5a) How do I know there is a problem – what evidence do I have?

It is easy to go to the coach and give vague outlines of a problem, but you need evidence. This evidence helps convince the coach that you are serious and gives a baseline to know when you have resolved the problem. The difficulty is that since most coaching problems are intrinsic rather than extrinsic, you need to look inside for evidence – something that we are not really encouraged or trained to do.

5b) How will I know when it is resolved?

Coaching is a finite activity – if you don't have a clear end point, the risk is that you go on and on, never quite graduating and closing down the engagement.

CONTINUE

6a) Have I tried this before (unsuccessfully)? If so, why did it not stick?

So often coaching has little to do with the activity under consideration. In many cases it is about someone's inability to stick with change (note the huge failure of diets). If you have a habit of not sticking with change then be honest and tell the coach about it. That way it can be considered as part of the coaching cycle.

6b) What are the triggers that might cause me to revert to old habits?

Triggers are external factors that cause slippage and reversion to old habits. Think about the things that have historically caused you to slip and share them with the coach. You can then prepare a plan to deal with them before the coaching partnership is closed.

Table 13.1	Continued

Questions

CLOSE

7a) **When complete, how will things be different for me?**
Coaching that focuses on the change itself will struggle to stick. Coaching that can focus on the end value has more chance of lasting. Don't think about overcoming the fear of presenting to the senior managers because all you will picture in your mind is a row of cold faces. Instead define how life will be richer at the end and hold on to this as a future anchor.

7b) **What problems might I have in maintaining the change once the partnership is closed?**
One day the coach will leave. Think about any difficulties you might have when this happens and deal with them while the coach is around. Don't leave it to the last minute to panic and start calling them for help.

By ensuring that the client considers these questions before meeting with the coach, a clear signal is offered about the goal to deliver a sustainable change. The challenge to the client is, 'Be serious about yourself and the coach will be as well.'

However, it is important to understand what can often happen when the client is asked to undertake work prior to the first session. Three of the more common outcomes include the following:

- They smile enthusiastically and agree to do the work but never quite find the time to look at the questions. This is often an indication that they did not really want to be coached, and maybe just wanted cuddles and a simple solution provided on a plate. As such it is a good outcome because it has saved wasting both players' time.

- They take the questions away, begin to consider them and find that they don't actually need the coach after all because the answer has surfaced in undertaking the investigation. This is coaching in its purest form – where the coach has helped the client with a minimum of effort and cost on both sides.

- In working on the questions the client can answer half of them but really struggles with the other half. This is great because it helps both them and the coach understand where to focus most of the energy.

Hopefully the client will fall into the latter two options. But if you find that the first has happened you will have saved yourself a great deal of time and effort.

Reaping the anticipated benefits

Although some clients might view these questions as potentially off-putting and painful, they should be viewed in the same way as mock exams. This pre-test process serves a number of purposes. Clearly the major one is to help filter out those who 'will' from those who 'won't' or 'can't'. But they also have other benefits. They help grow confidence in the client's ability to deliver; they take a lot of the fear away from the process, and they help to identify areas where improvement can be taken prior to the real event – all of which in a coaching context can add real value for the coach and client. Coaching is a very expensive personal development option and anything that helps limit the level of pain and cost for both players must add value.

Possibly one of the most important aspects of the pre-coaching questions is that they help begin the transfer of ownership. The soft underbelly of coaching is the idea of power distribution. It is far too easy for the client to end up in a subordinate role, where the coach is viewed as a god, guru or genius, someone who has the wisdom and power to solve all the problems. This leads to a huge array of issues. One we have already considered is the notion of dependency. As with any cult leader, once the leader dies or disappears the cult will wither and fade because the people are in most cases overly dependent on the leader. The same thing can happen (and often happens in the sporting world) when the client ends up in a subordinate role. Once the coaching is over, old habits return and all the good work fades because the coach is no longer around to support the good work.

ff The soft underbelly of coaching is the idea of power distribution. 刀刃

Use of the pre-questioning process helps reduce the chance of this happening because from the outset the coach is saying to the client, 'you own this', 'you must do the work' and 'you must own the solutions'. As a consequence the questions help move the coach's role from that of content expert to process guide and as such one they can withdraw more easily.

Honest coaching

However, as with all things, there is a cost – and this cost falls to the person who wants to be coached. If the client believes they want to be coached, they must be prepared to commit time and energy to the necessary pre-work. However, in most cases this pre-work isn't of an extrinsic nature where they have to carry out research or write papers. It is significantly harder than that. They need to look inside and be honest with themselves.

Because often all the great coach is doing is asking them to look in the mirror — and asking them why they don't do certain things. The question is, will the client be really willing to allow the coach to shine a light into dark caves that they might be happier to bypass? This can involve emotions which both parties need to recognize are OK as part of learning.

In answering the pre-questions it is easy for the client to fake it and not tell themselves or the coach the truth. Honest use of the questions will help them really address many of the issues that have prevented peak performance in the past. In surfacing issues that they have suppressed or not bothered to look at, the coach can really help turn poor performance into peak performance – something they both wish to achieve from the coaching partnership.

The manager as coach

Of all the topics that raise most discussion on the courses we run, the most common and significant one is the idea of line manager as coach. Run a search on the web under this idea and you will be flooded with courses and papers that expound these ideas, generally voicing the following aims and goals:

- How do you motivate employees to go after 'the ripest fruit' or drive for the dream that seems beyond their grasp? You do it by coaching. Coaching is what cultivates employee growth, not to mention employee loyalty.
- Coaching others well is an essential skill for a successful manager. Coaches need to be able to inspire and empower others to develop goals and achieve their personal and organizational objectives.
- Coaching includes motivating team players, transferring knowledge, inspiring cooperation and shaping behaviour.

Clearly it would be foolish to suggest that these aims are not both within the remit of the manager and eminently desirable. However – and this is a very big however – I do believe that they can be mutually opposing and difficult to achieve. Now before the cries of heresy are shouted in my direction, I do not suggest that the manager cannot employ the skills and style of a coach to help lead and direct the team members. Where I do have a question is around the idea of an individual being both manager and coach at the same time.

It can be all too easy to confuse the role of coach and manager, and indeed I am sure that many managers will vigorously defend the idea that they coach their people as part of their managerial role. Much of this is because they will use the same or very similar underlying capabilities. However, the critical issue is that of accountability and authority. In a managerial position, ultimately the manager is (normally) accountable for delivering the agreed objectives and their salary and bonus may well be dependent on such achievement. Additionally, they typically have a formal mandate as part of the contract of employment to authorize the staff member to take an action and as such sanction or discipline them if they fail to take the necessary action. Whereas in the terms considered in this book, the coach does not take on board accountability for the outcome of the client's goals and should not be in a position where they can use their authority to pressure the client to take action. The moment the coach either becomes accountable for the outcome or strives to exert their authority over the client, then de facto they are no longer a coach and they have become a manager.

This key differentiation separates coaches from managers and this is important because it defines and bounds how the coaching relationship is managed. Referring to the model introduced in the first part of the book (Figure 13.4), the manager is tasked to manage the resources and deliver the necessary performance, whereas the coach is employed to help the client help themselves, and while this may be a performance improvement, it is often more focused on the release of potential.

A key problem then is that apart from moving along the performance-potential line, the manager has to make the difficult shift from giving extrinsic solutions to the person and instead help them to find intrinsic

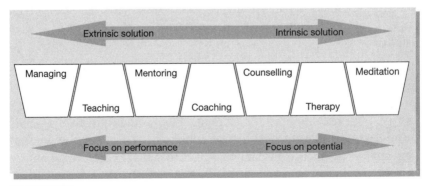

Figure 13.4   Coaching continuum

solutions and so look within. This can be difficult for the manager on a number of levels:

- They are used to giving answers and this has developed into a habit, such that they don't even realize it is happening.
- They might feel a loss of status because they are not offering the solution.
- They might not believe that the person is capable of discovering a solution themselves.
- The manager may be looking at their ability to help people by coaching them and hence a robust and rapid solution will help them look better.
- They might disagree with the client's proposed solution and want to override it because they 'know' it is not the right answer.

A prime example of the difficulty this can surface is when attempting to teach a partner or child to drive or play a sport. It seems eminently sensible that I should attempt to help Joe (my son) to learn to drive. I can drive and have passed my theory test again recently so understand the Highway Code; he wants me to show him to save money. But the moment we get in the car all the motivational and facilitation theories I have learned over the last 20 years go out of the window. For some reason I turn into the command freak from hell and he turns into the child of two who screams and sulks when they can't get their own way.

One of the core reasons for this can be found in the roots of role conflict. With our defined roles comes a set of responsibilities. Some of these are on the surface in that they are clearly defined, whereas others are shadow expectations that people assume but don't tend to talk about. When we look at the two roles of manager and coach, many aspects of the roles do overlap quite comfortably. The idea of helper, guide and teacher can fit into both aspects with ease. However, there are aspects where the two can be in conflict.

If we look at a dictionary definition of the manager, many of the common words include 'someone who controls, directs, measures or is in charge of an asset or resource'. Along with these words comes the ultimate issue, which is an explicit responsibility and accountability for the delivery of a service or product. So if something doesn't get delivered, the manager is responsible and can lose their job. Now it might be nice to manage people using human processes and techniques, but there may be times when the manager has to say things that are unpalatable to the individual.

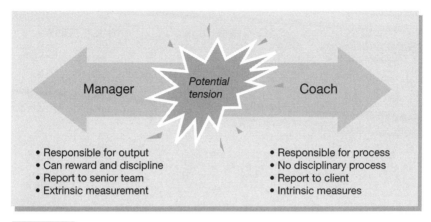

Figure 13.5 Manager as coach tension

This potential for real tension between the two roles can be seen in Figure 13.5 where the underlying differences in the two roles are shown. A real and tangible example of this for me is one client group where the managers were tasked with doing so many 'coaching sessions' per week to meet the corporate targets. One of the managers admitted to me that these weren't really coaching sessions they were just 'back-door bollockings' – a chance for the manager to highlight where the people were going wrong and pointing out what needed fixing.

Now this is entirely valid in a managerial role, but in that sense it is performance management, not coaching. Both roles have a place in the managerial role, the problem comes where the manager or the team member loses sight of which is in play at any time. The end result is shadows, confusion, game playing and the potential for coaching as a role to end up denigrated and derided. Because no matter how much coaching the manager does, they still have the power to sack, discipline or make the individual's life hell. I am just not sure how this fits with the idea that the coach is there to be an objective guide and helper.

The final problem is the manager-coach migration comes back to the choice pillars mentioned at the outset (Figure 13.6). The argument is that the client must make three choices: to decide what to be coached and invite the coach to help; to be serious about their stated intent to make a change; and to have a desire to be self-sufficient once the engagement is complete. Now imagine the manager who suggests to a team member that they could do with help on a topic and that they are happy to coach them to help resolve it. Bearing in mind that the manager controls this person's career, pay and overall

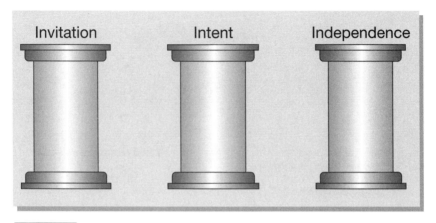

Choice pillars

happiness at work, the chances are that the team member will present a radiant smile and say what a great idea that would be. On the surface all is rosy, but at a shadow level:

- Invitation: There is no invitation by the client for help as it is imposed.
- Intent: The client doesn't really want to do it anyway and they will just fake it while the manager is around.
- Independent: Since there is no invitation or intent, we can be sure that any improvement is unlikely to be self-maintained.

So, the tension is that while the manager believes they are helping the person to help themselves, the simple fact that they have a significant influence over that person's career and life really does suggest that on the surface we might see coaching but in reality it is sitting on a layer of shadow management.

If the choice is to act as both manager and coach then I suggest that the following are considered:

- Understand the philosophical and practical difference between a coach and the manager using coaching tools. I can use coaching techniques to help my children, but I would be very wary of being their 'coach'.
- If the manager does decide to act as 'coach' then set up a process whereby the client understands when either role is in place. Try to eliminate role confusion and conflict by focusing on role clarity.

▪ Define a clear contracting process so that issues surfaced during the coaching process do not cross over and impinge upon the day-to-day activities (in reality not an easy or realistic process).

▪ Ensure that the senior team understand that both roles are being used, and any implications for the business – for example, increased time needed to coach or private spaces.

▪ Try to ensure that the client really does want to be coached and that they are not just doing it as a means to pacify the manager.

These suggestions do not resolve the problems highlighted when the manager also wants to act as a formal coach, but they might ease the journey where it needs to happen. However, my suggestion is still for the manager to hopefully use the coaching techniques to aid their managerial style – but to avoid wherever possible taking a more formal coaching role with team members.

14

Epilogue

Thanks for taking the time to explore the 7Cs framework and tools covered in the Collaborative Coaching process. I hope that it has given value to you. For me, writing the book has allowed me to be selfish and take some time to research further many of the ideas that seemed to be of value to the coaching community. It has also helped to reinforce my belief in the principles that underpin the ideas in the book.

Of all the ideas offered in the book, maybe the one that is key to the whole science and art of helping others is that coaching is about choices. As I started in the book talking about the choice point, the job of the coach is to help the client manage these points, change how they choose and ensure that the new direction is held true and that slippage doesn't occur (Figure 14.1).

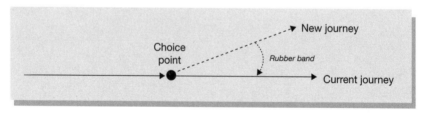

From outset to completion, the coach's role is to help the client make the right choice. I hope that some of the ideas in the book will help you to help your client make choices and help you make choices in your life as well.

I am always keen to review and refresh the 7Cs framework and tools, so please drop me a line if you have any thoughts on the content of the book.

Mick Cope
mick@wizoz.co.uk

Index